SIMPLIFY THE FUNNEL

The Ultimate Guide to
Streamlined Marketing Success
for Online Business Owners

ANT HODGES

"What Ant Hodges has created is a permission slip to abandon complexity and embrace what actually works. His MVF framework has transformed how I think about customer journeys and conversion. If you're drowning in funnel complexity, this book is your lifeline."

Ronsley Seriojo Vaz, Computer Scientist, Entrepreneur, Author, Speaker.

"Ant Hodges delivers what every online business owner needs—a clear, effective, and human approach to marketing. Simplify the Funnel® is the antidote to overwhelm, and a must-read if you're tired of complexity without results."

Mel H. Abraham, Money Mentor & Author, USA Today Best Seller, Building Your Money Machine

"As a Sports Vision MD Ophthalmologist, I have been buried in terabytes and terabytes of written and online information about how to build my business to serve athletes. Simplify the funnel® has come to the rescue and has shown me a clear path that makes sense, is not overly complicated and is most importantly doable without taking over my life! I wish I had this book sooner, not only would it have saved me a great deal of money, but more importantly a great deal of time which is our most precious commodity."

Daniel M. Laby MD - Assistant Clinical Professor of Ophthalmology (fmr), Harvard Medical School

"Ant Hodges has studied with the best marketeers on the planet. Everything that he has learned he has distilled into this book - his own take on marketing a business"

Kevin Wright – Founder, Ninja Investor Programme and Amazon #1 Bestseller - Recycle Your Cash

"Too often in business we over complicate things and confuse our customers. Ant's Simplify The Funnel delivers actionable insights on how to scale your business whilst simultaneously making it simpler, easier and more effective - genius!"

Steph Turton, Founder of Handbagholic

"Simplify. An easy word, but in digital marketing it can seem unattainable. Kajabi.com, the leading creator-commerce platform has powered over $9 Billion dollars in revenue generated by creators all over the world that believe simplicity is possible, and Ant Hodges is leading the charge. Ant has packed this book with his from-the-trenches playbook of what is working for creators today, and will continue to work, no matter how complex the digital landscape becomes. In the world of ai, authenticity is currency, and simplicity is the path forward. Set yourself free from complexity, we are rooting for you!"

Jonathan "JCRON" Cronstedt -Board Director, Kajabi.com (former President), USA Today Best-Selling Author of Billion Dollar Bullseye

"Here's the truth: Simplicity scales, and Ant Hodges is one of the brightest minds on simple real-world marketing strategies that actually work. If you're tired of funnel hype and want a smarter, simpler way to grow, read this."

Graham Cochrane - USA Today Bestselling author of Rebel: Find Yourself by Not Following The Crowd

"A refreshing read in a noisy world. Reading this inspired me to do more but with a simple mindset and when you're an entrepreneur that's often a challenge! Ant breaks down the practical steps to help any business owner or individual building a personal brand and you'll finish the book fired up and ready to take action!"

Jenni Field - Leadership Credibility and Organisational Communication Expert - Author of Nobody Believes You

"If you're done with overcomplicated systems that leave you stuck, "Simplify Your Funnel" by Ant Hodges will change how you look at your business, it's a goldmine of practical models and frameworks. Ant strips away the noise and gives you clear, practical steps you can actually use, by boosting your confidence and showing you exactly what to focus on. Trust me, this is one of those books you'll keep coming back to as you level up your business."

Advita Patel, Director of CommsRebel & CIPR President 2025

Published in the United Kingdom and United States of America

Paperback: 978-1-0687609-3-8
Hardback: 978-1-0687609-4-5
Ebook/Kindle: 978-1-0687609-5-2

YOU
YOUPRENEUR PRESS

Published by Youpreneur Press - www.youpreneur.com

For direct contact with the author, use the following details:

Ant Hodges, HodgesNet Ltd, Workshed Unit 5 Carriage Works, London Street, Swindon, SN1 5DB (United Kingdom)

Instagram: @Anthodges - Email: service@hodgesnet.com

www.anthodges.com - www.simplifythefunnel.com

To the entrepreneurs wanting to serve and make a difference in the world...

It's time to reject complexity as strategy.
Embrace the power of doing less, but better.
Your business deserves clarity.
Your life deserves freedom.
Your success demands simplicity.
The simplify revolution starts here.

Contents

Foreword

When Ant asked me to write this foreword, it didn't feel like a formality. It felt like one of those full-circle moments that reminds you why you started.

Ant's been part of the Kajabi story for years... not just as a customer, but as a believer. He's flown across oceans to show up at our events. He's organized meetups to bring people together. And more than once, he's pulled me aside to remind me what really matters.

I still remember standing backstage at a Kajabi event, minutes before walking on stage. Ant walked up and handed me an Old Fashioned... because he remembered it was my favorite. No fanfare. No pitch. Just a thoughtful gesture from someone who gets it.

That's who Ant is. And that's why this book is worth your time.

Simplify the Funnel isn't another funnel-hacking playbook. It's a reality check from someone who's been in the trenches. Someone who's watched complexity masquerade as strategy... and seen too many entrepreneurs burn out chasing someone else's system.

As the founder of Kajabi, I've seen behind the curtain of thousands of digital businesses. The ones that win? They strip it all back. They stop building for the guru and start building for the customer. They get out of their heads and into action. They don't chase perfection... they chase momentum.

That's what this book gives you.

Ant's Minimum Viable Funnel™ and SEED Marketing™ model are simple, not simplistic. They're human. They're clear. And they're built on one core belief: that marketing doesn't have to feel gross to work.

If you've ever looked at your funnel map and wondered how it all got so complicated... if you've ever delayed a launch because your "automations" weren't quite perfect… this book is your permission slip to get back to what matters.

Whether you're just getting started or scaling past seven figures, this is a roadmap built on clarity, integrity, and action. Not gimmicks. Not fluff. Just what works.

You're in good hands with this one.

Kenny Rueter
Founder, Kajabi

Introduction:
Everything Changes Today

If you're tired of trying to implement complex marketing funnels that drain your money and energy, bringing you minimal results, then…

STOP!

…you've got the right book in your hands; everything changes today.

I've been in this marketing game a long time and have seen so many people trying to educate entrepreneurs and business owners about marketing funnels who have little or no experience in getting any results for themselves. Don't get me wrong, there are some amazing marketing service providers that can actually help clients build out successful funnels, but they are often very hard to find. Was sad to see many of my previous clients in my agency career coming to us with a completely wrong attitude to building out a marketing funnel for their online business. It was not their fault. There are just too many marketing people selling services based on things that used to work in marketing who are blind to what actually works, because they are following the teaching of funnel marketing books written a decade or more ago. That's why I had to write this book.

From being on the front line in the agency world for over twenty years, I have seen first hand what is working and what's not. Things go in cycles. Tactics that worked yesterday fall out of sync with others that are more successful at generating leads and sales at any given time. In this book I'm going to introduce you to things that have stood the test of time because of the power of simplicity.

Many of the most successful entrepreneurs on the planet have enjoyed sustained growth in their businesses and very lucrative paydays by doing one thing. Simplifying.

I called this book "Simplify the Funnel" because that is what almost every online business owner that I come across needs to do with their marketing efforts - simplify.

The conversations from many clients over years have gone something like this...

"Can you build this funnel blueprint I just spent $5,000 on?"

...or...

"Please copy her funnel exactly - she is making millions and I want the same set up to make me millions too!"

Suffice to say that almost all of the times that we've implemented work for clients inside my agency from businesses that have requested work like this, nothing worked out of the box in the way that the client would hope that it would. So, I stopped doing the work requested like this.

Yes, when you buy into a high-ticket program from an expert or guru that you believe to have the answers you are looking for. Their promise often comes with a packed funnel ready for you to build into your business.

I have spent so much money myself, investing in the same

business-building programs, and found many of the ideas to be so complicated that all of the budgets that the client would spend on having someone build out the funnel, leaves nothing in the pot for marketing. And if they tried to do it themselves, it would take months for them to implement - if they didn't burn out from the insane level of work and hustle needed to get it working.

Instead of implementing the blueprint that I was often presented with, the clients from my agency that succeeded the most were the ones that allowed me to build out what I thought would work best for them.

With my streamlined approach to building out simple funnels, I've seen many move from making nothing online to making their first sale and growing businesses right into multiple seven figures. The focus was on using only essential elements in marketing funnels for maximum impact, then building on what is working.

I'm giving you everything in this book around these simplified ways of working.

After I cover off some marketing fundamentals about where funnels came from and why I am against the idea of building out complex funnels, this book will dig into a concept that I call the **Minimum Viable Funnel™ (MVF)**. This is what I've been working with in my business and with my clients since 2012. It's an approach that has out-trumped many other complex funnels, coming into its own in the new post-pandemic era that we live in now.

The MVF is designed to help you achieve quick wins and create the right foundations to build on for long-term success. It's about fast implementation on smaller budgets so you can get to market as quickly as possible and have a budget left for marketing.

Many have tried to copy my framework and methodology. Some of my previous students and clients simplified more than their funnel and are now helping others to simplify their businesses and their lives too. For me, this is amazing - the more that I can know about this, the better, and I champion them. I will be the person in your corner championing you also if you implement, get results, and share this message of simplification with those in your world.

Simplification of your marketing will enable you to be able to get better results, faster.

No book can promise to give you all the information, the magic silver bullet, or a push-button solution to earning millions. So, to be clear, this book is not that. If you expected it, put it down now.

But, if you want to learn strategies that you can implement yourself, see first-hand the difference it can make to your marketing and sales efforts, and help you to quickly get out of the trap of just spinning your wheels in your online business - let's continue. I will give you a clear pathway to market your business effectively and get some traction ***FAST***.

One thing, before we jump in, understand that there is work to be done now and continual effort needed to build a successful business. Overnight success is possible and often shows itself after seasons of hustle.

Knowing how to build out an MVF in your business will get you onto the right track towards success - however you define it. And then you can leave the hustle culture behind you. The only thing you need to bring to the table is a strong work ethic.

Inside many of my training programs and with my clients, there's one thing that I've said time and time again that has been the secret to my success, and I'll share it here with you now...

Implementation is the ONLY superpower you need to succeed

If you're open-minded, ready to unlearn some of the old

thinking, and are prepared to learn something new and focused on getting things done, then let's go!

Here's to your success

Enjoy

PS... you can find resources to help you implement what you'll learn in this book at **www.simplifythefunnel.com/resources**

1

The Evolution of Marketing Funnels

The concept of the marketing funnel was not created by some marketing guru in the 90's

Few realize this, but the fact is that marketing funnels have been around for over a century, evolving from simple direct-response advertising concepts to the overly complex, multi-layered technology-based systems we all have access to today. But here is the thing - complexity does not always equal effectiveness. In fact, it often leads to confusion, both for the business owner and the customer.

I remember buying access to a high-ticket marketing program and system that offered me a complete marketing machine that I could implement into my business with a few clicks. It was a system developed by an online marketer that many people will know and love, and a system that he trained many people to be able to implement for others - even ending up creating a certification program for all the elements around it that could help people position themselves as expert marketers - to then make money selling marketing services.

The process of getting this machine into my CRM and marketing system was easy - it was simply a couple of clicks. It installed over thirty different email sequences directly into my marketing engine. There was automation triggered from almost everything, which led the prospect in the funnel down one path or another, depending on their behavior and the action they took. In essence, the machine would work them through the funnel automatically based on what they would click on and even what they would ignore.

On the surface of it, it looked amazing. This guy's team had built out an entire marketing system that, after paying a princely sum, was in my business within minutes.

There was then a challenge. Every email needed to be read, updated, and changed to accurately reflect my personality, brand, and values. There were literally thousands of emails to update.

After going through a number of the email sequences and rewriting them all to be in my tone of voice, thinking that when I was finished I could invite people into my marketing funnel and they would be converted into customers so easily, I stopped.

It was when I got to one email sequence called "the throat grabber." The purpose of the emails in this sequence was quite straight, and to the point, and with the name it was given, it was designed to grab the prospect by the throat and tell them that they needed to take action. It felt like the sale was being forced. This was not something I wanted to implement in my business. It felt manipulative. It felt sleazy. The name of the email sequence was enough for me to go, "No, thank you."

The marketing funnel that I launched did not have that sequence deployed, and to this day, nothing of this kind graces any of my marketing systems. In fact, after a few months of running the whole machine, I saw that just three of the sequences and only a handful of the automation was working in my business. They were helping me to generate 6-figures a year without all the complexity that the machine I had installed offered.

I learned that just because one guy has made millions of dollars implementing a system that included all these sequences, the automation, and even some questionably named processes, I could see that I didn't need to have them all in my business to be able to succeed. From that day I chose to take a different path, against the grain of what everyone else was teaching online. One that followed principles I was taught in my early days of learning about business and marketing - right back at school.

The Birth of the Marketing Funnel

The marketing funnel concept was not created by some marketing guru in the 2000's with the dawn of the automated CRM and funnel-building system; it actually dates back to 1898 when E. St. Elmo Lewis developed the AIDA model. This simple and very linear approach served marketers well for decades, providing a foundational understanding of how consumers move from awareness to purchase. It still serves marketers and businesses well today if they follow it.

Despite the fact that Lewis developed this so long ago, many modern marketers and so-called experts have developed what they believe to be their own unique methodologies and frameworks without acknowledging the original source of their learning.

The truth is, nothing is more effective than this tried-and-true model when it comes to understanding consumer behavior.

Yes, we can create marketing funnels, campaigns, and promotions that have a few more than four steps in them, but the principles of anything implemented into a marketing funnel today have the DNA of AIDA running through it, albeit a genetically modified version of it.

There is no way on this planet that I can add to or take away from the framework of AIDA to make it an easier concept for us to understand and implement in our marketing strategies. What I can do is bring some context to it and unpack some thinking of how it applies to your business in today's modern marketing world.

Phase 1 - Attention

The first step in any marketing funnel is to grab the attention of your potential customers. Although "Awareness" is a term often used to describe this phase, it was not part of the original model developed by Lewis. Attention is the correct term to use here, and in today's noisy, fast-paced digital world, getting a consumer's attention is harder than ever. They are constantly bombarded with messages, advertisements, and content, trying to get some of their limited attention.

As marketers, we have to find a way to cut through this clutter. This means finding creative ways to stand out. Whether it's through eye-catching visuals, a clever hook, or an unexpected value proposition, your goal is to break the noise barrier so that you can get noticed.

To gain attention, you have to understand what resonates with your target audience - what grabs their interest and makes them stop scrolling or listen to what you have to say. Think about where your audience spends their time and how they consume information. Whether through social media, search engine marketing, or even offline channels, your initial goal is to get in front of the right people with a message that stops them in their tracks.

There are many ways we can do this, but it has to start with taking time to understand your potential customer's frustrations, fears, and aspirations. If we try and spend some time walking around in their shoes, we can create hooks and value-driven content that will get their attention and see us as an expert who can help them to achieve what they are looking for.

I will share my SEED Marketing™ model in this book that shows you the exact way to get the attention of your potential customers when everyone is begging for their attention also.

Phase 2 - Interest

Once you've captured the attention of your potential

customers, the next step is to sustain it by generating deeper Interest in you, your content, and ultimately, your product or service.

This is all about deepening your connection with them - almost like the first few conversations you might have with someone you have just started dating. In life, as it is with marketing, it's not enough to just make someone aware of your existence - you need to have and offer something that intrigues them, something that makes them want to say, "I want to continue this conversation" with this person.

The best way to do this is to demonstrate value or solve a problem the consumer has. Right off the bat, before the sale. If you can give someone results in advance of buying from you, their interest will deepen because they get value from you and your content. It's like investing in the bank of goodwill - you can make a withdrawal at some point in the future.

Use tactics like storytelling, educational content, inspirational content, or providing useful information that speaks directly to your audience's frustrations and aspirations.

Here's my number one tip for creating content that will peak interest - when planning content for your marketing, ask yourself the question: "If I were my potential customer seeing this, why should I care about this piece of content?"

If you can answer that, then it's something you can create content around that will move your potential customer from just having some awareness of you to having an active interest in you, what you say, and what you have to offer.

Phase 3 - Desire

As the person who has entered your world becomes more interested in you and what you are about, your goal is to cultivate Desire. You need to move beyond presenting information to creating an emotional connection.

Consumers should not only be aware of and interested in your product - but they should also want it. This is where understanding your audience's deeper motivations and pain points comes into play. People will justify purchases with logic, but this is after the sale. They will ask themselves things like "Did I get value?" and "Does this do what I expected it to do?" However, most buying decisions that come before the act of actually giving you any money will be driven by emotion.

Emotions influence everything from the brands that people choose to the products they buy. Whether it's the excitement of owning something new, the relief of solving a pressing problem, or the aspiration to achieve a particular lifestyle, emotions are the driving force behind desire.

If you are selling a luxury product, it's not just about selling the item itself; you're selling the feeling of exclusivity, status, or self-indulgence. When selling a practical solution, such as a time-saving tool, you're not just offering efficiency - you're offering the promise of the feelings that will be felt in the future - the peace of mind that comes with having more time for the things that matter.

Emotional drivers are far more persuasive than a simple list of features or logical explanations.

To create desire...

- Focus on ways that you can help the person you are speaking to through your marketing and feel the emotions that align with the outcome your product or service provides.

- Highlight how it will make their life easier, more enjoyable, more successful, or how it will get them the result faster.

- Use powerful imagery, success stories, and language that stirs their emotions, helping them envision a better future with your product or service.

When you tap into these emotional drivers, you're far more

likely to turn interest into genuine desire.

There is a caveat and a kind of request that I want to bring here, though: **Don't be a Plonker!** (This is the affectionate term used by Del Boy in the TV show Only Fools and Horses when he refers to his brother Rodney when he has been a bit of an idiot)

The old-school Internet marketers of yesterday would pose on the hood of their Lambo or in front of a big house in a paradise setting, showing off their lifestyle and promising overnight riches. Some of these Internet marketers were found to be nothing but fraudsters, and some were even sued by organizations like the Federal Trade Commission (FTC) in the US and Trading Standards in the UK for misleading consumers because of the way they used to fake the success they showed off.

In recent years, I have seen less of this kind of marketing, possibly because of the fear of getting into hot water with the authorities. But, recently, when I was watching a webinar from an AI agency, it was like I was back in the year 2005.

The owner of the company was sitting, presenting from an office with a tropical beachfront view from the window behind him. It looked nice, and I thought nothing of it. The content of the webinar was interesting, but there was little

I could take away in terms of actionable content, so my "Plonker" radar was up, and I started to look at everything I could see on the screen.

There were no photos or personal items in the camera angle used. And after about an hour, when he stood up and the camera followed him outside to the driveway of his house, everything looked sterile and completely unlived in. Yes, I know some people have a minimalist way of living, but nothing showed that this was his home.

While out on the driveway to this beach mansion, he started his pitch, and I couldn't help but say out loud, "What a Plonker!"

"All of this could be yours," he said as the camera panned around and then walked amongst the six cars parked up in front of him. A white Rolls Royce, two Ferraris, a Mercedes G Wagon, and, yes… a Green Lamborghini!

When he sat on the hood of the Lambo, I saw the chat blow up, and I just laughed. I had lost all focus on the presentation and the pitch.

So many people dropped comments into the chat like, "He didn't just try and close me while sat on the hood of his Lambo, did he?" Everyone was switched off; many said they were leaving the webinar, and I did, too.

Online, there was a whole heap of chatter about this marketer in some of the groups I was part of. The house he shot the webinar in was borrowed from a real-estate friend and was on sale for $6.2 million, and all but one car was rented for that shoot. The only car that was his was the 9-year-old G Wagon.

Fake it until you make it does not cut it anymore.

Desire does not look the same for everyone. You need to work out what the desire of your audience is and mirror this in how you present yourself. Yes, many will want the lifestyle you have, but some won't. If we play the lifestyle card, we need to be genuine with our lifestyle and success.

The world has become such a smaller place since the days of the Internet marketing boom in the early-2000's. Fake looks fake, and even when it doesn't, it will get found out.

Phase 4 - Action

The end goal for any funnel or marketing campaign is Action. You have done the job of grabbing your potential customer's attention, sparking their interest, nurtured desire, and now it's time for them to act - whether that's making a purchase, signing up for a service, or taking the next step in your customer journey. The action phase is where you turn potential customers into actual customers.

No potential customer will buy, though, without clear and compelling calls to action (CTAs) - they are essential. Whether it's a "Buy Now" button, a sign-up form, or a phone call, you need to make it as easy as possible for the customer to take that next step by creating a conversion event so that they can engage with you somehow.

Reducing friction in the buying process - by streamlining the checkout process, minimizing steps, or offering incentives like bonuses - can make the difference between a conversion of a sale and a missed opportunity. But here's where many business owners hesitate - asking for the sale.

I heard it said so many times, "I don't like to sell" or "I don't want to come across as pushy." Here's the hard truth - if you don't ask for the sale, you won't make any money in your business. Selling isn't about manipulation or pushing people into something they don't want, it's about offering a solution that you believe can genuinely improve someone's life or business.

If you've taken the time to build a great product, establish trust, and nurture desire, then asking for the sale is simply the natural next step. If selling is something that you struggle with, then this is a huge mindset shift you need to make.

Selling should be an invitation, not an imposition. You're

giving people the chance to act and solve the problem they've been struggling with - you're offering them value. And you deserve to be compensated for that value.

Think of it this way - if you're not confident enough to ask for money in exchange for your solution, how can your potential customers be confident that your product or service will meet their needs? They need to know you believe in the value of what you're offering and that confidence comes through in how you present your call to action.

Break the fear of asking for money by focusing on the transformation you provide for the customer. Selling is simply a necessary part of doing business, and when done with integrity, it's a win-win for both you and the customer.

"The aim of marketing is to know and understand the customer so well that the product or service fits him and sells itself."
~ Peter Drucker - The Practice of Management

AIDA is the basic form of any funnel. With anything in human nature, people think they can add to it to make it better, and they have tried to. With the dawn of the funnel building and the access now available to technologies that were previously reserved for the blue-chip companies with big budgets, it seems that complexity has become the norm.

The Rise of Digital Marketing and Funnel Complexity

As the online business world became more complex, so did our funnels. The world went crazy in terms of activity to program systems and funnel flows that tried to take into consideration every possible action that a lead would take when they entered our funnel. What we tried to do was to say that if someone did something, didn't do something, clicked, bought, or anything else in between, we would create an action based on that trigger.

This was before the age of Chat GPT and the mass infiltration of AI into our marketing that now helps us to predict this kind of activity in some instances today. As you read this, there is no doubt in my mind that the technology would have moved on again since the time I was tapping on my keyboard to write this.

Within marketing funnels, we added stages, created loops, and developed complicated systems designed to capture every possible customer interaction. The thinking was to create the system once so that we could simply continue to pour leads into and it would do all the work for us.

The thinking was that the funnel would build relationships with people, add value, and convert people into customers by selling for us. If we designed a complete funnel, tested it, and it worked, then often, it would be left alone to run all day, every day.

The data that the funnel would give us would tell us if it was working or not. With all the tracking systems available, we have access to more data than ever before, this can be a good thing and a bad thing. Clicks, opt-ins, opens, purchases, views, interactions... the list of things we could measure was endless and ultimately became the focus of any funnel builder.

The question is, do we really need it all?

Many marketers and business owners seem to have fallen into the trap of thinking that more stages, emails, and touchpoints will automatically lead to more sales. This thinking often comes from stats and studies that marketers share with you, which show customers often need multiple touchpoints before making a purchasing decision.

In my time selling off-the-page advertising and by studying buying behavior online, I have seen people present anything between seven to twenty-three touchpoints before a prospect becomes a customer.

Stats like this can be helpful to see that we should not always expect a prospect to buy on the first interaction with us, but the preaching of stats like this has led to a rise in the need to make marketing more complex. "We need more touchpoints" is the thinking. As a result, we get endless sequences of emails, ads, and digital engagements.

While it's true that consistency and follow-up are critical components of successful marketing and sales, we have to recognize the difference between **quantity** and **quality**. The number of touchpoints alone does not guarantee a sale - the nature of those touchpoints is what truly matters.

In today's online world, where customers are inundated with automated emails and cookie-cutter marketing machines that they are copying from one guru to the next, people are increasingly seeking genuine, human interaction. The human touch - personalized communication, authentic conversations, and real empathy - is what sets successful businesses apart from those simply churning out generic content in a broadcast fashion and are just focusing on the numbers, not the people.

Automation, the use of AI, and technology all have their place, of course. They an essential tools for scaling your marketing efforts and ensuring that you remain top of mind. But when automation is overused, it becomes nothing more than noise for you and your customers. Customers can tell when they're just another email address on a list, receiving a pre-written message that lacks personal relevance. Worse still are the emails with fake levels of scarcity or emails pre-written that say things that follow open cart or webinar offers like "many people are jumping in, are you in" – when, in actual fact, this email was written long before the cart has opened and potentially the offer may have had no sales converted yet.

I am a firm believer that automation should support your marketing efforts, not replace the human connection that builds trust and loyalty. It's almost impossible to be totally genuine, full of integrity, and human when you automate everything to the N'th degree.

A personalized follow-up email after a discovery call, or even a direct message that addresses a prospect's specific questions or what they said in the conversation you have just had, carries far more weight than an automated sequence of generalized messages aimed at indoctrinating me into your world. **It's about showing potential customers that you care about them individually, and they are not just numbers in a funnel.**

Businesses that prioritize these human touchpoints, whether through one-on-one communication, thoughtful customer service, or personalized outreach, are the ones that will see lasting results.

Instead of thinking, "more touchpoints equals more sales," we need to simplify things and rethink what type of touchpoints we're creating. Ask yourself things like, "How can I foster genuine relationships with my prospects?" and "How can I bring some real authenticity into every interaction, whether automated or not?"

When we focus on the quality of engagement rather than just the number of engagements, we build deeper connections, stronger trust, and, ultimately, more loyal customers.

Complexity often leads to confusion, and confusion kills conversions. Post-pandemic customers craved human interaction more than ever - and the online marketing world changed forever. Even before the world was hit by lockdowns and restrictions, causing people to feel disconnected and isolated, customers were saying that they wanted simplicity when it comes to the sales process.

"55% of consumers are willing to pay more for simpler experiences."
~ Global Brand Simplicity Index 2018, Siegel+Gale

So, let me repeat what I just said, in case you missed it:

Complexity often leads to confusion, and confusion kills conversions.

It's time to simplify. It's time to flick the switch in our minds and create an easy path for our prospects and potential customers to be able to buy from us. In turn, we create a much simpler way to manage our business too. Is this not a win-win?

Simplifying for Maximum Impact

The 3% Rule, as put forward by Jeremy Miller in his book Sticky Branding, says that at any given moment, only about 3% of your market is actively ready to buy.

This means that 97% of potential customers are at different stages of awareness, with 7% considering change but not yet ready to act and the remaining 90% either unaware of the need or unwilling to purchase.

If just over half of consumers are willing to pay more for simpler experiences, as Siegel+Gale's research shows, then the real opportunity lies in capturing that 10% who are already primed to buy or who are considering change.

Simplifying your funnel through approaches like the Minimum Viable Funnel™ (MVF) is key to efficiently moving these active buyers toward action without overwhelming them with unnecessary steps.

Are you open to doing a little math with me and seeing

how this might play out? Completely hypothetical but I want to illustrate things here for you.

Don't worry, I have done all the workings out. I want to show you the potential in just one niche to make simplified marketing really work.

Imagine you are marketing an **Online Parenting Course** aimed at parents with children under five. The course is priced at $497. You know that parents are often searching for solutions to common parenting challenges and might be open to your course.

Let's work the numbers according to the data that is available online:

- When we say 55% of consumers are willing to pay more, we're not talking about this proportion of the total market; we're talking about the customers who are already open to making a purchase.
- Miller explains that around 3% of a niche market are active buyers, and around 7% intend to make a change in terms of a problem or challenge they have
- This means that 10% of a potential niche is open to buying at any time.

- Taking 55% of this 10% (those willing to pay more for simplicity), it means that 5.5% of a niche that is in buying mode is willing to pay for simpler experiences in the buying process.

- UNICEF's "The State of the World's Children" report suggests that there are approximately 660 million children under the age of 5 in the world.

- We can estimate that there are 1.6 parents per child, drawn from the United Nations "Population Division Reports on Households."

- And we can see that the Int. Telecommunication Union (ITU) suggests that only 67% of people have internet access.

- This leaves us with around 710 million parents of children under 5 who are likely to have internet access.

- 5.5% of these 710 million parents equals 39.05 million potential buyers in this one niche.

- If your marketing and sales efforts convert just 0.1% every year from this number, that means you could be looking at annual sales of $1,940,785, with 3,905 people paying you $497 for your one training product.

If we niche down, stop trying to be all things to all people, create a product specific to the exact challenges of a market and then position it as a direct offer, you will get sales.

This online parenting course will be relevant to a percentage of the niche that is out there ready to buy, so why complicate things and get them into a million touchpoint funnel when people are willing to pay for simpler experiences?

If you were to put them into a complicated sales funnel, with endless emails, upsells, multiple steps, and automated sequences, you put friction into the sales process, increase the decision density of the funnel and prevent people from buying when they are ready to.

The MVF strips away these complexities, focusing on a clear, direct path that resonates with those who are on the verge of making a decision.

With the MVF, you aren't just catering to your customer's attention span; you're also making it easier for them to trust your product, engage with your content, and make a purchase decision. By removing the barriers and reducing the cognitive load that comes with complex funnels, you're more likely to capture and convert those who are already primed to buy.

So, Why Do Complex Funnels Fail?

As a previous agency owner, helping many business owners to grow their online businesses in the creator economy, I have seen the results that have come from engineering complicated funnels. And if I am honest, the times we did pander to this worldview of complicated means more sales, things didn't work.

Hindsight is a wonderful thing - not! In seeing the online world change so much in the last ten years or so, I feel kind of bad for the way in which my agency used to offer services to clients, where we followed their lead (and the training they had bought from others), implementing the systems and processes of the gurus out there that were just so complicated. I wish we had been stronger and stuck to our convictions as a team. One of the reasons for writing this book was to set my stall out and say, "There is no room for complicated here - we simplify the funnel!"

After looking back at some of the abhorrent failures and some of the funnels that could have performed better - as it wasn't all doom and gloom - here are the top five reasons that I saw funnels fail.

1. Complex funnels are difficult to implement

Business owners often become paralyzed by the complexity

of funnels and systems. I can't count the number of times I saw clients fall into "analysis paralysis," endlessly planning, tweaking, and micro-managing their funnels but never fully launching them.

The more stages, technology integrations, and touchpoints we added, the more overwhelming it became - not just for us as the service provider but also for their audience. While the intent was always to build an all-encompassing machine, the reality was that most of these funnels never saw the light of day because they were just too complicated to execute.

In retrospect, a streamlined funnel would have been launched far sooner and would have allowed us to optimize through real-world feedback rather than endless pre-launch fine-tuning. This is why I developed the Minimum Viable Funnel™ framework and why this book exists.

2. Complex funnels are expensive to maintain

Complex funnels require multiple tools, so many pieces of software, subscriptions to this and that, and often have many connected platforms linked together to function properly.

I've seen clients who feel that they need to subscribe to a CRM, an email marketing platform, a video or media hosting service, a landing page builder, a webinar service, and a few other third-party integrations just to get a single funnel running. All of this didn't just increase costs; it also made troubleshooting an absolute nightmare. The more tools that we plugged into the process, the more technical issues arose. And every time something broke, or a system went down, whether it was an API integration failure or a payment gateway glitch, it caused delays, frustration, and additional costs.

The burden of maintaining such a setup was often unsustainable, and many clients abandoned their funnels after realizing that the cost-to-reward ratio - the investment in getting it all set up vs the money they were making on the other end - just wasn't there. My answer is just to go to **www.anthodges.com/kajabi** and sign up for the one platform that does it all.

3. Complex funnels confuse customers

The confusion that complex funnels created for customers was awful when presented with a plan to implement. As an agency team often followed instructions from clients to have funnels built out with multiple upsell pages, down-sell offers, follow-up sequences, and retargeting ads, thinking that the more options that were added, the better. In fact, the opposite happened. Their customers became confused, not knowing what the next step was or why they were being offered another product when they hadn't even decided or even consumed the first one.

We need to do so much education and re-training for the clients that we worked with in our agency to try and have them agree and allow us to create funnels that are seamless, clear, logical, and pressure-free. When your customers are presented with too many options or steps, they can get overwhelmed, lose trust, and are more likely to drop out of the process entirely. A confused customer won't buy - simplicity sells.

4. Complex funnels are hard to optimize

I remember when we used to build these grand, multi-layered funnels, only to realize later how hard they were so tough to optimize and improve. With so many touchpoints, emails, and sales stages, pinpointing what was working and what wasn't became our biggest headache in the agency. Was the problem with the landing page? The email sequence? The pricing? The upsell offer?

When there are too many variables, it becomes nearly impossible to find and know where the issue lies in a funnel. I've had funnel plans presented to me from clients, with 100's emails, automation, and touchpoints that they wanted to be implemented -simply because the high-ticket training that they have subscribed to and purchased told them to implement it all.

Even when trying to pare some of it down, when implemented, it never performed well simply because diagnosing weak points was a nightmare. On the odd occasion that I did raise a concern or point out a "leak" in the funnel, it was often seen as me questioning the client and their judgment on the purchase they made for that high-priced guru-led training they told us to follow and implement - headaches all around!

When we were able to implement simpler funnels with fewer stages, it allowed us to clearly see where leads were falling off and make data-driven adjustments quickly and efficiently, then build more and scale up if needed - some clients were just happy with simple funnels; with one or two offers that were making money every day.

5. Complex funnels are inflexible

The business world evolves quickly. The online world is even more so. This means that anything we do in our marketing and sales activity must be agile, and we should always be able to adapt fast.

Complex funnels tend to be rigid and so big that they make it difficult to pivot when market trends change or when new opportunities arise. Whether it was updating a product offer or responding to competitor shifts, we often found ourselves tied down by the complexity of these systems. Even a small change could require hours of reworking multiple sequences, landing pages, automation, and ad sets. As a result, many funnels couldn't keep up with the pace of change. The inflexibility of overly complex funnel systems led to missed opportunities, as businesses were too bogged down in the intricacies of their funnels to pivot when needed or the distractions of another opportunity to add elements into their funnel to cash in.

Simpler is Better

By reflecting on these failures and challenges in almost fifteen years of helping clients build and launch funnels, it's clear that simpler is better. Those that I worked with and implemented simple funnels at speed succeeded more than the complex builds that my team and I were involved with.

Building a streamlined, customer-focused funnel not only increases the speed at which you can go to market but also makes it easier to implement, enhances the customer experience, and allows for easier optimization.

Funnels should guide prospects toward a decision and allow them to make it, not confuse them or bog them down with unnecessary complexity, pressurizing them into a sale.

When you build simple funnels, you can do so at speed if you need to pivot because you are responding to data, market conditions, or world events.

Sarah's Story...

Back in 2017, I had a client, Sarah, who ran a successful yoga studio in Bristol (United Kingdom). She came to me after investing £7,000 in what she called a 'complete marketing system' from a well-known guru. The funnel had 17 different email sequences and a flow that suggested she needed 9 different offers to link up upsell pages and complex behavioral triggers that would send people down different paths based on every little action they took.

After three months of trying to implement this system, she was frustrated and overwhelmed. Her team spent countless hours just trying to understand how all the pieces fit together. When we analyzed her results, she had spent more time and money setting up the complex system than actually connecting with her potential customers. The few leads that did come through were confused by the multiple offers and constant upsells.

We scrapped the entire thing and started fresh with a simple three-step funnel...

- A free yoga pose guide
- A £27 beginner's program
- And her flagship £997 yoga teacher training.

Within the first month of launching this simplified approach, linking these three offers in her own MVF, she enrolled 12 new students in her teacher training program - more than she'd converted in the previous three months combined.

The Need for a Simplified Approach

Attention spans are shorter than ever. Many studies have shown that this post-pandemic shift, with much of the blame being attributed to "Zoom fatigue."

"...prolonged video conferencing is more exhausting than in-person interactions due to factors like constant close-up eye contact, reduced mobility, and the cognitive load required to process non-verbal cues in virtual environments. This leaves people mentally drained and less able to focus for extended periods" ~ Stanford University, 2021

Before the pandemic, attention spans were shrinking too, even shorter than a goldfish's!

"...the average human attention span has dropped to just 8 seconds,"
~ Microsoft Attention Spans Research Report, 2015

Combine these eight seconds with the post-pandemic screen fatigue, and it's clear that capturing and retaining attention with online marketing, long drawn-out funnels, and when using tactics like webinars and a video sales letter (VSL) is more difficult than ever before.

From my previous experience of running many campaigns and building many funnels in my agency, I hope that I have unpacked for you what I have seen in terms of the impact of complicated funnels, marketing machines, and blueprints. Not only will the challenges I shared with you a moment ago rear their ugly head, but it's the fact that some of the training or books that you might have bought and consumers were created, written, and published over a decade ago or more.

People simply don't have the mental energy to engage with convoluted processes. We need to capture attention quickly and guide prospects through the funnel efficiently. That's where the MVF comes in.

Again, the MVF is not about dumbing down your marketing; it's about **stripping away unnecessary complexities and focusing on what truly drives results**. It's about being strategic, efficient, and most importantly, human.

Where screen fatigue and shortened attention spans dominate, human touchpoints in funnels that are genuine and empathetic make all the difference to the success of any funnel build.

By simplifying your funnel, you reduce friction for your audience, guiding them toward action without overwhelming them with endless steps. Complex funnels over-promise and under-deliver, but simplicity that connects on a human level delivers in a world of fleeting attention.

The Promise of This Book

I hope that you can see that there is a need to simplify. And that you're ready to learn from me exactly how to do that in your online business.

In the following chapters, we'll dive deep into the components of the MVF and how you can implement it in your business. I will unpack some of the other methodologies and frameworks that I have developed over the decades of being a geek in this world. Together, we'll explore:

- **The SEED Marketing™** model for creating engaging content - understanding that audience building must be your number one priority when you want to be seen in a crowded marketplace.

- **List-building for today's online world** - how to move beyond freebie hunters and have Profitable Lead Generation campaigns instead.

- **The core components of the Minimum Viable Funnel™** - and how to implement them into your business.

- **My Selling Without Selling™ sales technique** - that is responsible for my successfully selling to 90% of triaged sales calls into my business. This is all about real and authentic engagement.

Remember, simplicity is not about being simplistic. It's about focusing on what matters most and executing it exceptionally well.

"Simplicity is the ultimate sophistication."
- Leonardo da Vinci

Are you ready to simplify your funnel and amplify your results?

Let's do this then!

2

The SEED Marketing™ Model

"There is No B2B or B2C: It's Human to Human"
~ Bryan Kramer

I remember when I was a child, going on a school trip to London. My friends and I often used trips like this to just mess about and have fun. There wasn't much learning going on. Only fleeting memories remain of some of these trips, but I do remember one thing that has become part of the foundation for my mindset when doing anything.

When masons and architects in the 19th century started to build some of the amazing buildings you see in London, the cornerstone was the first stone to be laid. A lot of time and effort went into making sure it was positioned correctly. It had to have the best foundations, it had to be the right shape and size, and it was always squared up to the exact position that it needed to be - often lifted and set back down again many times to get it right.

It's been this way for hundreds, if not thousands of years. It wasn't just those tasked with the construction of some of London's now-famous landmarks that had to ensure they laid the cornerstone correctly. Buildings all around the world, going back generations, all had an initial cornerstone laid at the start of construction. This was because the rest of the structure was aligned against the cornerstone and measured from it. Without it, buildings would not be level, square, or built to the dimensions in plans and drawings given to the builders.

I say all this so you can understand the context and importance of what I am now going to say...

Visibility is the cornerstone of effective online marketing.

Everything in your business, the success you strive for, and the challenges you encounter along the way will all come down to how much attention you get in the marketplace - you only get that by being visible.

In the creator economy, in almost every niche that I come across, you need to be the one who is seen, not just a faceless brand. People do business with people. You need to show up in their world. But showing up in someone's world isn't enough to build a successful business.

You need to find ways to demonstrate your expertise, share your uniqueness, add value and find ways to build a relationship with your audience. You are not selling a course or a membership; you are selling transformation, and that comes from people buying into you and you leading them to that goal they have or ambition that they have craved. This is what **SEED Marketing**™ can help you with.

It's All About Human to Human

If we agree that showing up and being visible is not enough and that by adding value and serving our audience, we all start to move away from some of the language that marketers use, such as Business-to-Business (B2B) and Business-to-Consumer (B2C), and instead look to the idea of Human to Human (H2H).

This is not a new thing I am talking about here. I first read about the idea of moving toward an H2H point of view when I was introduced to it by Bryan Kramer in his book *There is No B2B or B2C: It's Human to Human*, published in 2014. Regardless of the type of business, at its core, all marketing and sales come down to human relationships. He suggests that the old distinctions between B2B and B2C models ignore the simple fact that behind every business transaction is a person making decisions based on emotion, trust, and connection.

The H2H approach aligns perfectly with the shift we're seeing in customer expectations today, particularly online. People want to feel valued as individuals, connected with others, and not just as another transaction or number in a funnel. This is so important in today's digital world, where simplicity and authenticity are more valued than ever.

Human interaction in marketing builds trust and long-term relationships by appealing to emotions, which is part of the first step when any consumer makes a buying decision.

I love the idea of H2H and am not just suggesting we start using it as a new buzzword - it's been around for a while now. What I'm saying is that we must shift our entire marketing mindset. We need to be more focused on empathy, authenticity, and creating genuine connections with our customers. This human-centric approach is the foundation of simplifying your marketing and using my SEED Marketing™ model to do all of this.

How the SEED Marketing™ Model Came To Be a Thing

The SEED Marketing™ model was born out of my own struggle with the complexity and time-consuming nature of content marketing. Coming out of lockdown in 2022, I found myself frustrated with the narcissistic approach many influencers were taking online. Things felt fake. There was a "look at me, look at me" attitude to many of them, and very few experts were standing out. I needed a framework that would help me and my clients build an audience that would differentiate us from others in our own niches, while staying true to who we were.

I remember sitting at my desk, staring at my 90-Day Marketing Planner that I created and used in the business with some clients. It is essentially a content planning calendar that I put together as a workbook that people can buy and use. I felt overwhelmed by the constant pressure to create new videos and social media posts when everything in the past seemed to create nothing more than a damp squib of buzz online rather than a tidal wave of inquiries. I knew there had to be a more systematic way to create and share content that actually served my audience.

The real spark came when I was asked to present a workshop on content marketing for an online summit in February 2023 - nothing like a deadline to get your thoughts into a framework when you must teach it! This event forced me to formalize the approach I'd been developing.

I knew that I needed something that wasn't just another

"post X times per day" formula, and it had to be away from everything to do with the new kid on the block that has been around for just a few months - Chat GPT - to focus on human, authentic content creation that would demonstrate how the brand owner was a real expert.

The framework I drew in my notebook has become something that has helped people create authentic, expert-level content without getting lost in the overwhelm of needing to create lots of content. That was what was holding me back personally in the first place: the thought of needing to create all that content. The framework I taught I had implemented for myself and my clients, and it was generating leads and sales, not just the growth of vanity metrics like followers and like.

It felt like I was cheating though. It sounded so simple that it felt wrong to teach this from the stage. I presented the SEED Marketing™ model, and it was well received. People could truly see that I was not adding to the noise of all the other marketers out there; this was different. I presented something new, simple, and repeatable as a process that would help entrepreneurs share their expertise in a way that felt genuine and delivered results.

The SEED Marketing™ model is designed to help you increase your online presence and attract, build, and retain the right audience by focusing on four key areas...

S - Shape Expert-Level Content

The first step in the SEED Marketing™ model is to shape expert-level content that positions you as a thought leader in your niche or industry. This isn't about showing off, and it's not about being attractive to your colleagues in your industry either - it's about providing real value to those who will potentially become your next customer.

Many people make the mistake of holding back their best insights and wisdom, saving them all for paid products or services. But in today's digital economy, being generous with your expertise is what sets you apart.

What I am saying is that there is a direct conflict with a lot of people teaching experts how to market themselves online. They say to never share the "How" as you can put that into a paid-for product and sell it after you share the "What" and the "Why" - my view, don't shy away from talking about the "How" in any of your content.

If you don't share it, they will just search for someone else who is sharing it and then the eyes are off you and onto the next person.

The thing to remember, though, is that it's not just about

what you are sharing either...

"Content is king, but context is God."
- Gary Vaynerchuk, Jab, Jab, Jab, Right Hook

Gary V reminds us that the secret weapon in content marketing isn't just what you create - it's understanding how and when you share it.

Expert-level content without proper context is like serving a Michelin-starred dinner on a paper plate - the quality of what you're offering gets lost in poor presentation. Creating content that your audience genuinely craves requires strategic thinking about three key elements...

- **The Message** - First, you need to carefully craft your core message, ensuring it provides real value and speaks directly to your audience's needs.

- **The Medium** - Then, you must consider the most effective format for delivering that message.

- **The Moment** - Finally, you need to time your content's release for maximum impact.

Without considering all three of these elements, you are gambling and hoping that the content lands in the right way. By being strategic, you can avoid some of the mistakes that I have learned along the way.

Just like Erica. She was a client who was an awesome business coach and growth strategist. Her writing was brilliant and detailed, but her blog posts, which reached up to a few thousand words every week, got virtually no engagement. Her site was getting found on Google, and she was getting visitors, but there was a problem.

We decided to email a short survey to her list and post links to it on social media in an attempt to find out if her message was landing well, if the medium she was producing it in, and if the moment it was published each week, was all aligned with how they wanted to consume content. The results gave us the answers that we were hoping for.

We discovered that those she wanted to reach were mainly consuming content during their commute - a time when reading long-form content wasn't practical. Erica continued with the writing of her detailed blogs, but we also pivoted to delivering the same insights through videos and audio. Videos were posted directly onto LinkedIn and she created a form of audio podcast that you could only get on her website.

Publishing the content every Monday at 7 am and moving into these two additional forms of content saw her engagement skyrocket. Erica's expertise had not changed, but we matched the context to her audience's preferences.

If your audience primarily engages with video content but you're solely focused on written blogs, you're not just missing an opportunity - you're missing the mark entirely. Your expertise deserves to be consumed, and that means packaging it in a way that fits seamlessly into your audience's daily lives and preferred consumption habits.

How to Shape Truly Impactful Expert-Level Content

Step 1. Identify Your Areas of Deep Expertise

This goes beyond simply listing your skills or experiences. You need to dig deep into your professional journey and identify the unique combinations of knowledge that set you apart. Think about the intersections of your experience - these crossroads often reveal your most valuable insights.

For instance, one of my clients was a former HR director who became a business coach. Instead of trying to compete in the saturated general business coaching market, she focused on the specific challenges of scaling teams while maintaining company culture - an area where her HR background gave her unique expertise. Her content naturally stood out because she could speak to both the strategic and human elements of business growth.

2. Develop Unique Perspectives on Topics in Your Field

Having expertise isn't enough - you need to have a point of view. This means analyzing common industry practices, questioning conventional wisdom, and developing your own informed opinions based on your experience and observations.

I encourage my clients to keep some form of "perspective journal" - even if it is just on their notes app on their phone. The purpose is to regularly write down their thoughts on industry trends, common practices, and recurring challenges they observe.

Over time, patterns emerge that help them develop and articulate unique viewpoints that challenge or expand upon accepted industry norms.

Tom, a financial advisor, booked a call with me to talk about his challenges with lead generation from LinkedIn. It was the main tool that he used for building community, but in fact he wasn't building community at all. He was cold messaging people, saying things like "It's so great to find someone like you - I'd love to connect" and in the second message, diving into pitch mentality.

He said to me, "That's how I was trained in a course I took earlier this year" - without telling him he had wasted his money, I simply said I think I know a better way. I took him through my SEED Marketing™ framework and showed him how he could show up as an expert, build relationships, and serve a community that would draw people to him rather than him being the hunter all the time. It transformed his business.

He started operating out of a mindset of creating real, authentic connections by serving a particular niche - Millennials. His LinkedIn following grew from just under 500 to 15,000 within 4 months, and inquiries became too much for him to handle on his own. This resulted in him having to take on two para-planners and another advisor. Growing the business by picking a niche and showing up as a real, authentic expert for those people.

Tom completely transformed everything about his content after adopting a new way of showing up on LinkedIn. Instead of cold-messaging anyone and sharing generic investment advice, he developed a compelling perspective on how technology was changing personal finance behavior in ways that traditional financial planning wasn't addressing, specifically addressing the need for Millennials to take note and secure a better future for themselves. He became the hunted.

3. Create and Share Your Own Frameworks and Methodologies

This is where you truly differentiate yourself. Your frameworks and methodologies are the practical manifestation of your expertise and perspective. They provide structure to your ideas and make them actionable for your audience.

Think of frameworks as your intellectual property - unique ways of approaching common challenges in your field.

These don't need to be completely revolutionary; they can be improved versions of existing approaches or new proven method combinations.

The SEED Marketing™ model you're reading about now is a perfect example. While human psychology hasn't changed, this framework provides a fresh, simplified approach to digital marketing that challenges the complexity many are teaching and promoting.

When developing your frameworks, focus on...

- Solving specific problems your audience faces
- Making complex concepts more accessible
- Creating memorable acronyms or names that stick

- Providing clear, actionable steps
- Including real-world applications and examples

Remember, the goal is to **DEMONSTRATE** that you're an expert, not just proclaim it. Your content should showcase your expertise through practical application, not just theory. When you consistently share valuable insights, frameworks, and methodologies, you build authority naturally without having to explicitly state your credentials.

The key is consistency and depth. Don't just scratch the surface of topics - go deep enough to demonstrate true expertise while still keeping the content accessible and actionable for your audience. Every piece of content you create should either solve a specific problem, provide a new perspective, or offer a practical framework for approaching challenges in your field.

Remember that "Perspective Journal" I mentioned a moment ago? This can help you shape and formulate your frameworks. The thing to be diligent with when keeping this kind of journal is always recording the source of the information you just made a note of.

I will often remember hearing things or seeing things online and then want to share them with my community or clients. There are still times that I can't remember where

I heard them from, so refer back to my notes on my phone and give the right attribution to what I am sharing.

I see many people sharing frameworks and methodologies that others have created online. Maybe that's because I am a prolific reader and consumer of content around my industry, and I can spot things that I have read or seen before. Some are attempting to try and pass off frameworks as their own, either deliberately or simply because they can't remember whom to reference. This could land you in hot water if you infringe someone else's copyright, even by accident.

AI tools like Chat GPT are prone to give you frameworks and methodologies in responses to your questions and prompts simply because it is regurgitating what it has learned – don't use that output as your own thoughts either. Only very recently did I see a marketer who was promoting a framework he said he had created but admitted to me that he used Chat GPT to help him create the content. I saw that it pretty much ripped off, word for word, part of The 5 Stages of Awareness, a copywriting framework popularized by Eugene Schwartz in his 1966 book called Breakthrough Advertising.

But, the talk about AI is enough for another book. In my view, use AI as an assistant not a replacement.

E - Engage Your Audience

Shaping great content is only half the battle. You need to actively engage with your audience to build real connections. And here's where most people get it wrong - they think broadcasting content is enough. You know, the "post every day" crowd of experts.

I've noticed after years of watching businesses try to grow their audience online...

The ones who succeed aren't necessarily creating the most content - they're creating the most conversations.

Engagement isn't just about racking up likes and comments. It's about creating a genuine two-way dialogue that builds lasting relationships with your audience. If someone likes your content and you ask a question, then they take the time to reply, do them the courtesy of replying back. Try replying with another question to keep the conversation going, too.

Think about it like this - would you rather have 100 followers who actively engage with you, comment and have conversations with you publicly, and eventually become customers... or 10,000 followers who scroll past your content without a second thought?

I know which I would rather have.

Creating Real Engagement

Let me give you a breakdown of exactly how I would focus on creating engaging content for your business if I got my hands on your social media...

1. Use Relatable and Interactive Content

Stop trying to be the perfect "guru" in your niche. The polished social media profile with all of those posed photos and highly designed and branded posts. Be real. In general terms, social media is about people sharing content on the go. This user-generated content style has some of the biggest levels of engagement because it is more relatable than aspirational.

I blame the Internet marketing sharks of yesterday for this confusion. You are the type that I shared about earlier in this book – the guy who rented a mansion and a history of expensive cars to try and portray a lifestyle that was aspirational to get more attention. This still works for some, but on the whole, relatable content is the thing that connects people far more than posing on the hood of a Lambo.

Be genuine and human, in other words. Share your real

experiences, including the challenges and setbacks. People connect with authenticity, not perfection.

When you're creating content, ask yourself: "Would this make someone stop scrolling and think, 'Finally, someone who gets it!'?" That's the reaction you're looking for.

When coming up with ideas for myself or helping brainstorm this with coaching clients, I will often think of things like...

- Showing true human emotion in every post
- Sharing lessons from my own journey
- Asking thought-provoking questions
- Creating polls and surveys
- Encouraging people to share their experiences
- Shooting quick videos in different locations

It's not hard to be relatable and create content that will be interactive in terms of getting a conversation going, you just have to think outside of the box of the polished influencer mindset and just show up as you. Spending time becoming a content planner and prepare your content ideas in advance, this will help you create in a constant way.

More than anything else, when you bring emotion into your content, it connects at the right level.

In a sea of AI and automated content that doesn't include emotion, you will stand out. People want to be able to connect with you when they engage, and if you express emotions that they're feeling, that they have felt in the past or they desire to feel in the future, they will stay engaged.

2. Respond Promptly and Meaningfully

Here's something I learned the hard way - a delayed response is often the same as no response. When someone takes the time to comment on your content or send you a message, they raise their hand to connect.

Don't just drop a quick "Thanks!" Instead, respond to the comment and finish with a follow-up question, or share an additional insight and then ask them their opinion on it.

When I say I learned the hard way, there was a short video (a reel) that I posted on Instagram a few months back. Someone commented on that post and asked a question – "This is great, Ant; how can we work together?" That is a buying signal if ever I saw one. But, the trouble was, I didn't see it. About two weeks later, my social media manager on my team highlighted it to me and said that I had not responded. I commented and then sent a direct message to the person, inviting them to book a call. The short response I got back was, "I found someone else as you didn't reply" – ouch!

Every comment and every engagement deserves more than just a like on that comment or an emoji thumbs-up response. Spark up a real conversation. Remember, every comment is an opportunity to deepen the relationship. It's not always an invitation to pitch though; remember that too.

3. Host Live Q&A Sessions and Webinars

Nothing builds a connection faster than real-time interaction. When you go live, you're not just sharing information - you're creating an experience. Your audience gets to see the real you, ask questions in real-time, hear their name mentioned in life when you say "Great question [Insert Name Here]" and truly feel part of a connected community with you.

I've found that even a simple weekly Q&A session, like the one that I host every Monday in my member community, can transform your relationship with your audience. They stop seeing you as just another content creator and start seeing you as a trusted advisor.

Show up live, do the unscalable, build real connections.

The world is so quick to jump into evergreen and on-demand webinars. You can simulate a live start, have fake live chat showing up on screen with AI responses, plus you can eject people and filtering them out using AI for all the people causing issues or simply based on their comments and questions. If someone is willing to pretend to be live and be that disingenuous with simulated lives from the start, what else would they follow through on in the same way if I bought from them?

On webinars specifically, from all the campaigns I have run for clients and myself, live webinars have a higher conversion rate than evergreen, particularly when you are refining your message and presentation. When you have that dialed in, and it converts, consider doing evergreen, but don't fake it as live and always have a live option up your sleeve, even if it's a once-a-month date in your calendar.

4. Share Behind-the-Scenes Glimpses

People don't just buy what you do - they buy into who you are. It goes back to the H2H mindset we spoke about earlier and how sharing relatable content gets more engagement. Even big brands understand the need for relatable storytelling in their advertising and marketing.

One thing that works even better in the online business

niche is the sharing of behind-the-scenes activities in your business. It brings something different to the marketing that you offer and gives people a glimpse inside your business, humanizing it and your brand.

When you offer a sneak peek at the processes you use in your business, the practices you teach, and how you are implementing them yourself, this builds huge amounts of trust. You are being openly genuine and are demonstrating that you practice what you preach.

This is one of the reasons that I share how I do things within my business to my Membership Community and debrief on things like launches and campaigns to my Mastermind group. It shows the inner workings of my business and how I am applying exactly what I am suggesting they do in their business.

Other things that you could share from a behind-the-scenes perspective could be...

- Your workspace setup
- Your content creation process
- Your health and wellness routines (struggles and successes)
- Your planning sessions

- Your team meetings (if you have a team)
- Your wins AND your challenges

"64% of consumers want brands to connect with them on a human level." - Sprout Social Index

That isn't just a nice statistic - it's a clear indicator of what your audience craves. Ask yourself how you can connect with your audience, community, and audience in a real way by adding behind-the-scenes content so they can see the inner workings of your business. You'll separate yourself from those who just put on the "front" like many of the influencers out there.

Making Engagement Work In Practice

I am sorry to say that it takes time and effort. There is no one-click solution to get the engagement your brand and business need to make your marketing work for you. It's an unscalable activity that we need to find ways to systematise and put processes in place so it doesn't consume us. Here's what I recommend to my coaching clients...

Block out 30 minutes each day specifically for engagement. This isn't the time for creating content or planning strategies - it's purely for connecting with your audience.

"30 minutes" I hear you scream at the pages of this book. Yes. You can find the time. The doom scroll on social media that you get lost in, the soap opera that you tune into every day, or the Netflix binge planned for this evening - how about you take the time you would have spent doing that and use half an hour, and use this quickfire checklist of activity, to engage with your audience...

- **Respond to all comments on your recent posts** – reply in context to their comment and then finish by asking another question to continue a conversation.

- **Reply to relevant messages** – your Messenger inbox, InMail, or DM's could be hiding a seam of gold you just need to tap into (in and amongst the spam and pitching you get from others). Respond to the relevant messages and try to spark up a conversation that could lead to them asking to buy from you.

- **Engage with your audience's content** – It's not just your content that you should be engaging with, but your audience's too. Look at those that are following you; like and comment on their content. How would you feel if the people you follow and look up to took the time to comment on your content? That's exactly how your audience is going to feel when you do that on their content and this is only going to build more of a positive connection with you.

- **Join relevant conversations in your niche** – individual content that you can engage with is great, but getting into forums, groups, and other communities and adding your thoughts, help, and knowledge is like mining for gold. Where do your customers hang out online? Go in and answer questions and be helpful. You'll be seen by more than just the person asking the question, and who knows where that could lead.

The key to engagement is to **CONNECT** with your audience on a deeper level and **INVITE** them to take the next step with you – that could be as simple as answering a question or commenting, but here's the crucial part - that invitation should feel like a natural progression of the relationship, not a sudden pitch.

Engagement isn't just another marketing tactic. It's the foundation of building a sustainable, profitable business in today's digital world. When you focus on creating real connections, the sales and growth follow naturally.

E - Echo Core Values

I started life as a graphic designer in my teenage years, and then, in my early twenties, I started my first business – a branding agency called Creative Rush. One of the biggest parts of the job was to help clients understand what makes their brand unique, and it was far more than just the colors and logo they used. We often used to use the phrase "*Step Away From The Crayons*" in meetings, which is the title of a book co-written by Phil Parr and Alan Bright. The book talks about holistic branding and the need to go beyond just looking at the visual aspect of branding. Everything about branding, in my opinion, hinges on the values you hold as an individual and how they translate to your business. Values were the biggest talking point in all branding consultations.

Back in 2019, I was working with a client who was trying to be everything to everyone. When looking through their marketing, they would post motivational content, the next day technical tutorials, then switch to jokes and memes, even complaints and really negative posts about companies and the services they had undertaken. There was no doubt in my mind that their audience was confused about who they were and what they stood for. They have very little engagement despite posting more and more content because that is what their social media marketing company told them to do.

This is where most business owners and personal brands get it wrong; they think being good or talking about lots of different things would make people like them more. In reality, your core values aren't just some nice words to put on your website next to your vision and mission statement; they are demonstrated by everything that you say and do. They're your compass for every piece of content, every customer interaction, business decision, and the measuring stick for your audience to gauge who you really are.

Why Values Matter More Than Ever

In the noisy online world that we all run our businesses in, people aren't just buying your products or services - they're buying into your values.

"Your brand is what other people say about you when you're not in the room."
- Jeff Bezos

What I would add to Jeff's quote is that your values are WHY they're talking about you in the first place. There are four ways to make your values work for your business.

1. Define Your Non-Negotiables

Start by identifying 3-5 core values that truly represent what you stand for.

But here's the key, don't just pick nice-sounding words because they might look good on some kind of motivational poster in the office or because someone else is using them; choose values that you're willing to stand by even when it costs you money or opportunities.

It's about the integrity of you and your brand here, together with what you want people to really see, feel, and experience when they come into any kind of contact with you or your content.

The last couple of years have been interesting in my career. I am sitting writing their book as someone with mild dyslexia, remembering all those thoughts that said I would never write a book. I am no author, yet I am writing it.

I am stepping into a new level of brand building for brand Ant Hodges, away from the marketing service provider world that I have been in for almost two decades, so I needed to do this work myself.

There were a number of key questions I have had to ask myself, and questions that have been tough to ask at times that did challenge me on a value level. They needed to be asked to work through the pivot away from running an agency towards the coaching, training, and speaker arena, where I could use all the knowledge and wisdom I have gained over the years to serve more than just the customers in my agency.

Here are three of the big questions about my values I had

to work through...

- If **Authenticity** as a value matters within the expert business and creator space, will you share failures alongside your successes?

- If **Simplification** is a core value that you want others to bring into their business and life, are you willing to turn down complex, high-paying projects and retained services if people ask you to deliver them?

- If **Education** about simplifying is crucial for every online business owner, are you prepared to put the work in to create human and truly authentic content you will then share on video, podcasts, and other content marketing, rather than take shortcuts and let AI do your content creation jobs?

Let me say that my answer to all three questions is a 100% resounding yes, and I need to stand on those answers moving forward. These three questions, and some others, have essentially helped me to refocus and define for myself the purpose and non-negotiables around my personal brand as I step into this new and exciting world away from a career in the agency world.

My question to you is, what are your non-negotiables? And what questions do you need to ask yourself to test them?

2. Stay Consistent Across All Platforms

Here's where some drop the ball - they act one way on Instagram, another on LinkedIn, complain like anything on X and then are completely different in their email marketing also. Your values should shine through regardless of the platform.

Whilst different platforms do have different ways that their users engage with content, your message and the values you put on display should be the same across them all.

Think of it like this: if someone found your content on any platform, would they instantly recognize it as yours? Not just because of your logo, but because of how you communicate and what you stand for?

A lot of experts in the creator economy don't have personal Facebook profiles and essentially keep their personal lives out of the public eye. It's following the celebrity way of doing things. In a way, I see the merit in doing this, but I also feel that sharing your humanness is important, and you can choose what you post and how you engage on personal profiles. In my opinion, don't fear showing your life to the world. It shows you're more than a businessperson at the end of the day. But be consistent with how your content shows up and what you post.

3. Have a Visual Identity That Reflects Your Values

Your visual branding isn't just about looking good - it's about visually representing your values. When working with clients, we spend time ensuring their visual elements align with their core message. For instance...

- If **Simplicity** is a value, you don't need an all-singing, all-dancing website with all the bells and whistles.
- If **Innovation** is key, your visual identity should feel modern and forward-thinking not representative of a 1990's clip art logo or stages stock photo library.
- If **Authenticity** matters, you need to be using real images and real human-created content and have real conversations rather than letting AI take over.

Again, there are three things that I have checked in and worked on for me. How does your visual identity and how you show up reflect what you want to put out there into the world?

4. Niche and Stay in Your Lane

This might be the hardest part for many entrepreneurs, but it's so important. In fact, it's possibly one of the most important messages I want you to hear from everything else in this book, so I will make it bigger and bolder...

Stick to your area of expertise and let your values guide your content decisions.

It's such a hard thing to do, let me tell you. I learned this lesson the hard way. While I was running HodgesNet as an agency, I was so tempted to jump on every trending system, software and strategy to help clients. I wanted to find a way to offer all the services under one roof. But I realized, it's better to be known deeply for one thing than shallowly for many things.

As a team, we were growing, and I brought in a team to look at various things. In the early days, it was all about keeping websites up to date in WordPress, and the pain and torture of plugins breaking kept me up at night. Offering consultancy and done-for-you services to help people build out Infusionsoft systems and then link websites and shopping carts was even more of a headache. The list of "we can do that" services kept growing; I didn't even know what I offered sometimes.

It all changed when I got into Kajabi in 2012; it changed the game for me. During the pandemic, I knew I had to niche - to focus on just a few things that we could be world-class at rather than try to be that full-service digital agency. So, over time, out went public services and marketing for things like SEO, PPC, WordPress website design, using the white-label email marketing system we were reselling, Infusionsoft work, and eventually even video editing. We stuck with Kajabi, Facebook Ads, and social media.

Try and be all things to all people and you end up being master of none is what I am talking about here. When you don't have a niche, how will people see what you really do?

How to Echo Your Values in Practice

Making your values work in your business isn't a one-time exercise - it's a daily practice. It will require discipline, and I find that the accountability I get from my own coach and mastermind group helps keep me in check, too.

Here is a simple framework I use with my clients to help them stay true to their values while building their brand and ensuring this SEED Marketing stage of the process is stuck to.

1. Start With Your Value Audit

Take a good look at your current content and marketing efforts. Pull up your last month's social media posts, emails, and any other content you've put out there.

Now, rate each piece on how well it aligns with your core values.

Choose your own rating scale. You could use something like:

0 = Not Aligned through to 10 = Fully Aligned

Be brutally honest with yourself; this isn't about perfection; it's about awareness.

2. Create Your Content Filter

After you or your team has created the content you want to publish, and before anything goes out into the world, run it through these three simple questions...

1. Does this align with our values, or are we just chasing the algorithm to hope it goes viral?
2. Would our ideal client recognize this as uniquely us or would they possibly see someone else in this content?
3. Are we staying in our lane of expertise or getting distracted by shiny objects and trying to jump on a possible non-opportunity that we should be ignoring?

This filter isn't about limiting yourself - it's about being intentionally focused on what matters most.

And that is being absolutely true to who you are and what you do best in the world.

3. Monthly Consistency Check

Block time in your calendar every month to review how you're showing up across all platforms. Look for some important things like your consistency of message, alignment with your values, and also areas where you might be drifting from your expertise.

This monthly check-in is so important because if you don't have this time set aside, you could drift slowly away from the path you should be on. Your talents, skills, knowledge, and experience, together with your calling to serve where you are right now, need that check-in every now and then. I know I have throughout my career.

Block at least one hour a month to make that happen.

Echoing Your Values is Not About Perfection

Having your values fully on display and being true to them demonstrates your authenticity and your intention to serve. When you stay true to your values in everything you do, you will find that you attract the people you will love working with and love being part of a community with, and you'll naturally see people move away from you who aren't aligned with your values.

Your values aren't just part of your brand - they are your brand. Let them guide every decision, every piece of content, and every interaction. That's how you build not just a business but a legacy that stands for something meaningful.

Let's move on to the final piece of the SEED Marketing™ model...

D - Deliver Actionable Content

Over the years, I've spent many evenings poring over different clients' websites, their marketing content, social media accounts, blogs, and email funnels in preparation for a coaching call the next day. As a Funnel Coach, I've spent a lot of time helping clients refine the content that they're putting out there to make sure that it gives their leads, customers, and their wider audience exactly what they need to be able to fix the challenges that they have. Ultimately, the reason that any of us have email lists or customers is because people felt like we could deliver a result in some way, shape, or form.

I was reviewing a client's content library on a Sunday evening as I had a call at 10 am the next day. I went through her blog posts, social media, and email... as much as I could. She had tons of great information, but something was missing. Her audience wasn't taking action. Very few clicks from emails, no clicks from her blogs to her offers, plus videos and social media content that was getting exposure but had little engagement. Her audience was consuming content like Netflix bingers, but only a few were taking any further action.

I saw a glaringly obvious mistake that she was making. And it's a mistake that most content creators make when they're thinking about creating content for their marketing. The focus of most of the content was on giving extremely valuable information rather than presenting a pathway to transformation, and it had very little emotion.

What I mean by this is that the content she was publishing was pretty good information but it was boring, had no energy and certainly no real human connection. She would back up some of the things that she said with quotes from industry studies and other publications, helping to position her as a true expert, but there was nothing in her content that could help those who are consuming it to connect with her, remember her or take any form of action and get a result.

I remember when I was working for an agency between my first business going bust and starting HodgesNet in 2011. One of the things that had really started to gain traction in the marketing world was the use of Twitter (now called X). I was recommending that we jump onto Twitter and start sharing the knowledge that we had around

SEO so that we could demonstrate that we were experts. The company's management said, "But we make money from our knowledge; if we give it away for free, we won't make any money." It was almost like I could see what was going to come in terms of expert industry. We now live in a world where experts truly demonstrate the value of their knowledge and help their audience to get a result by actually helping them get a result before they purchase anything.

I think it was a guy called Frank Kern who coined the phrase that went along the lines of...

"Show your audience how you can help them by actually helping them to get the problem fixed that they have, even before you try and sell them anything."

I've been following Frank for such a long time, but this one sentence has stuck in my mind over all of these years, and it has become the default position for many content creators who understand the need to do something radically different with their content.

If we think about it from your audience's perspective, your audience doesn't need more information. What they actually need are paths to implementation, the only ones you can offer as a subject matter expert.

I think many things have been clouded in the "coaching" and "expert" space, with some trainers suggesting that the only content you put out into the marketplace should be the "what" and the "why" without any of the how? This is the old-school way of thinking about information marketing. We now live in a world where people want to get a result fast. Information isn't a commodity that we can sell anymore. Information is everywhere.

This final piece of the SEED Marketing™ model addresses this all of this head-on. When people engage with your content, you should be able to help deliver a result, which will help them to respond to your further calls to action. It is the universal law of reciprocity. If you help them to get a result, they will see value in everything that you do and will want more.

An example of expert positioning content that delivers huge value and invites the next step would be something like a short-form video (and Instagram Reel or YouTube Short).

Here's how you could structure a 60-second video that demonstrates your expertise, gives some steps on how to do something specific to fix a problem that they might have, and then invites them to take further action.

This framework will make sure your content delivers in

its; value and is action-oriented, without just dumping information and being another person broadcasting information, for information's sake.

1. Hook (0-3 seconds) - Grab Attention

Open with a strong, curiosity-driven statement or question related to your topic. Something like "Most people struggle with [common problem]. Here's the fix!"

2. Identify the Problem (3-10 seconds) - Make It Relatable

Clearly state the issue that your audience faces. A relatable pain point is that it is concise and easy to understand.

3. Explain Why It Happens (10-20 seconds) – Shift Perspective

Give a brief reason why this problem exists or why people get it wrong. This could include a personal anecdote or an example of another customer or client.

4. Provide Actionable Steps (20-45 seconds) – The 'How-To'

Offer 2-3 quick steps that the audience can implement immediately. Keep it simple, practical, and results-driven. A simple framework for this could simply be...

- Step 1 - Do this.
- Step 2 - Avoid this mistake.
- Step 3 - Try this simple tweak.

5. Call to Action (45-60 seconds) – Invite Engagement

Encourage those watching to take action, whether it's applying the steps, commenting, saving the video, or checking out a resource by clicking your bio link. Keep it clear and benefit-driven.

Use This Framework in Other Content

The five-point framework I've given you there for a short-form video is just one way you can make sure that you're not only delivering expert positioning content and value for your audience but you are inviting them to take the next step. The same framework can be applied to other forms of content. It's not strictly limited to short-form videos.

Emails, blog posts, even longer format videos and things such as podcast episodes can use the same exact formula. Our content will be seen as far more valuable when we include specific ways in which our audience can take action and walk down a path of transformation rather than just consuming information.

Guide Them to The Next Step

You have delivered value in your content, enough for someone to take action, but as humans, we need to be told, told again, and sometimes told again before we actually do anything or take action. Don't think that one call to action, in one piece of content is enough for you to be able to get the result you're looking for. Repeat the same call to action in multiple pieces of content that you create. Telling someone something multiple times will increase the likelihood that they will remember it and act upon it when they hear it next, as it's more familiar.

There are so many studies that show people need to hear things seven, thirteen, or even up to twenty times before though take some kind of action. There is no hard and fast rule here, but when creating your content and you want to create content that delivers value to your audience as well as a result of them taking further action, repetition is going to be your best friend.

Remember, particularly within social media, content is there for a fleeting moment. You need to repeat the same topics and messages over and over again. On a platform like YouTube, however, this content tends to live in an Evergreen position. You'll find that the content continues to be viewed by people over and over again if it's of value and the platform sees that there is engagement with it.

Three Ways to Make Sure Your Content Delivers for You and Your Audience

Guiding somebody beyond your content towards a specific offer that you might have can be a little bit tricky at times. The easiest way to think about this is that the offer must be an absolute no-brainer. It must be an extension of the content that they've seen to help them go deeper into the subject matter or to get the result faster than the useful path to transformation that you've detailed in your content. Let me break down, in four simple steps, exactly how to deliver content that drives real results for both you and your audience.

Step 1 - Create Clear, Compelling Calls to Action

This isn't just about adding a "Click Here" button at the bottom of the blog post or a link in your social post. Every piece of content you create should lead naturally to a clear next step. Think of it like having a conversation - you wouldn't suddenly change topics mid-sentence, would you? It needs to flow. Start with your content planning. You need to make sure that you link your content directly to specific problems you solve, and maybe even problems that only you can solve, using your expert framework.

Then, make your call to action feel like a natural next step. Focus on one clear action per piece of content. Tell your audience what they're going to get if they take the next step as well. They need to see the benefits before they take any action.

Step 2 - Offer High-Value, Actionable Content

The key word here is "actionable" - every piece of content should give your audience something they can implement immediately. It doesn't have to be the entire solution.

It could just be the first step in the process of being able to get the result. If they take this first step and achieve some kind of result, they're further forward than they were before they even saw your content.

This builds trust and shows you can deliver results. One step towards their goal is one step away from the problem that they had.

To make sure that all your content is actionable, think about asking yourself a number of questions when you review the content you've created...

- Can someone take action on this today?
- Have I broken down the steps clearly enough?

- What result can they expect?
- How will they know it's working?

If it doesn't pass the sanity check from your own mind in terms of being able to take action, then maybe we need to reword or repurpose the content in another way.

Step 3 - Make Implementation Easy

This is where most content falls short. It's not enough to tell people what to do or why they should do it; you need to show them how to do it, and it needs to be easy.

As I said a moment ago, we don't have to give everybody the entire pathway to transformation; we can just give them the first step or the first few steps. Living in a world where we only share the "what" and the "why" without any "how" keeps us firmly in the mindset of the Internet marketing guys of yesterday who were just selling information and not transformation.

Things that you can include that deliver on this could be...

- Implementation checklists
- Templates and frameworks
- Examples and case studies

Step 4 - Follow Up Consistently

Your delivery doesn't stop when someone consumes your content. I firmly believe that in an expert positioning world that we live in, where creators are sharing their knowledge online, the level of impact that we will have on the world will be directly proportional to the level of passion we have to help the person get the result they're looking for.

I'm not talking about the level of passion you have for your subject matter or even turning your "passion into profit" that so many talk about. What I really want you to understand is that if you're living in this creator economy and wanting to serve people, you've got to be sold-out and passionate enough to be present and serve your audience in such a way that there's almost no chance of them not succeeding, if they implement.

You can't take responsibility for their implementation, but if you've given them all of the tools and resources needed to be able to implement, then you've done your job.

Follow-up is essential for driving implementation and keeping engagement high. If someone comments, comment back and ask a question to keep the conversation going. If somebody opts in for something for free from your website, follow up in a way in which you can bring a human connection to the conversation.

And even consider producing more content that follows on from previous content – what I mean by this is doing a part two or a part three that follows on and helps people take the next steps they need on their journey towards transformation.

The Power of Consistent Delivery

When you consistently deliver actionable content that gets results, something magical happens. Your audience starts to see you not just as a source of information but as their guide to implementation and success.

Remember, the goal of the SEED Marketing™ model isn't just to attract an audience or build a following - it's all about creating real transformation in people's lives and businesses. And that only happens when you deliver content that people can actually use to get results.

Now that we've covered all aspects of the SEED Marketing™ Model let's look at how to bring it all together in your business...

Putting The SEEDs All Together

The SEED Marketing™ model works because each component reinforces the others. You shape expert content, which helps you engage your audience. As you engage, you echo your core values, building trust and recognition. Finally, you deliver actionable content that converts your audience into customers.

- **Shape** expert-level content
- **Engage** your audience authentically
- **Echo** your core values consistently
- **Deliver** actionable content that converts

By implementing the SEED Marketing™ model in your business, you could explode your awareness in a crowded niche online, position yourself as a true expert, and then see that increased following, engagement, and lead flow.

Implementing it isn't just about following these steps - it's about embracing a mindset of providing real, true value, building human relationships rather than letting bots try to do that, and consistently delivering on your promises.

In the next chapter, we'll explore how to move beyond simply collecting email addresses and start generating profitable leads. But before we do, take a moment to consider this one question...

How can you start implementing the SEED Marketing™ model in your business today?

3

Beyond Freebie Hunters: Profitable Lead Generation

Not all leads are created equal.

It's July 2009. My business has just been closed and put into liquidation. I'm sitting in McDonalds with my laptop and crying over my McMuffin! I'm trying to work out what my next steps are.

In the last seven days, I've had to make my entire team redundant, close my offices, hand back the car that I had used through the business, and try and grieve for the breakdown of the relationship between me and my business partner as he decided to abdicate all responsibility for the failure of the business and move to another country, leaving me to deal with all the fallout of the closure of the business - including all the debt.

Where could I turn to earn some money? I didn't have someone to help pay my mortgage and feed my kids and I needed to earn money fast. As someone who had left employment and started their own business, I sat there wondering, "Who would employ me?" I was not in a good place.

Having spent many years on the sidelines of the Internet marketing world, I thought that now was the perfect opportunity to jump into this world and start selling information online.

The first thing I needed to do... **build an email list.**

"Build your list!" – that's the one thing almost every internet marketer on the planet was telling me. Fast forward to 2024 (when I am writing this), and it's no different.

Every marketing consultant, guru, and funnel hacker says that you need to build your email list in order to have a successful online business. And in some sense, I don't disagree. **But what I do disagree with is "how" you build your list.**

Since the dawn of the Internet marketing world, list building has long been hailed as the holy grail. "The money is in the list," they say. Not only will you be able to market your own products to your list, but you'll also be able to market other people's products to your list. "Build your list and every time you send an email, you will make money"... that was the promise.

Between my business closing and jumping back into the entrepreneurial world in 2011, I had the privilege of working in an e-commerce agency and working with some top product-based brands. It was two years ago that I knew it was a path that I was supposed to walk to learn the art of selling products online. As an employed director of the company, I saw firsthand how e-commerce brands were **Positioning** and **Promoting** their **Products** in the right **Place**, to the right **People**, and at the perfect **Price**, the magical 6 P's.

I felt a call to jump in and help business owners take their knowledge and productize it into digital products. With products that would never go out of stock or gather dust on the shelves of warehouses like many e-commerce brands, I wanted to take the knowledge and experience of being involved with these e-commerce brands to sell knowledge-based products at a completely different level from the old-school Internet marketers.

List building seemed like a must-do strategy for any client that I was going to be working with. After all, it was the millionaire gurus of the Internet marketing world who were still telling me that everything revolved around building a solid email list.

Create your adverts, run those adverts to a squeeze page (what many would call a lead magnet opt-in page today), deliver a very simple 25-page PDF, and then blast them with emails to try and sell more products. That was what I jumped into work with clients on and what I was doing in my own business.

Was this strategy successful? To start with, yes. But over the years, I started to see things change. The problem was that much of the teaching of the Internet marketing gurus was not changing. There was still a sense that the only job you had to do was to build your email list.

After running my own list-building campaigns and those for clients I was working with, there's one thing I discovered...

Not all leads are created equal.

Thinking back to the days when I was implementing everything the Internet marketing crowd was telling me and trying to create e-books on subjects like powerboats, sports cars, and dog training, little seemed to work for me.

I spent all my days trying to get under the skin of Google Ads and list swap offers. Google ads would drive people to my squeeze page, and they would either opt-in or I would present my e-book with dozens of spun articles on the same subject, granting others a license to resell it (this is called PLR content – Private Label Rights). List swaps would pretty much be just the case of me buying an opportunity to send an email to somebody else's list in the hope that their list might be interested in what I have as well.

While these kinds of activities did grow an email list, the list quality was awful. It was full of freebie hunters wanting the information for nothing or people just wanting to take your content and try to sell it themselves to make money on the backend. More worrying, this was the kind of open-book strategy I was talking through and implementing for clients as well.

I remember those early promises from the Internet marketing guys that I had listened to... "Build your list, and every time you send an email, you will make money." I was trying to figure out what I did wrong. Personally, I had an email list I've nearly 40,000 people in less than 18 months. But every time I sent an email out with a promotion or an offer, I literally made nothing most of the time. A small $7 sale came in every now and then. But it was not like clockwork as I had been promised.

If it wasn't working for me, and it wasn't working for my

clients, there has to be something different that we could do. And that's when I tried something completely different.

After I decided to move away from trying to sell information in 2012 and actually create digital products that would bring real transformation to people's lives, it was like I had found a gold mine.

I'm talking about online courses, membership websites, and downloadable audio products. It was after reading the book "The Millionaire Messenger" by a guy called Brendan Buchard that everything changed for me.

With the knowledge that I had myself, rather than something I had to repropose from an article spinning, things started to change. I started to build a list of people who were interested in me serving them, and they started to buy from me.

I had created a video-based digital marketing training program with worksheets and downloads, and gave everyone who purchased, access to me so that I could answer any questions they had.

List building became a secondary priority for my business.

Selling became my number one priority.

The shift that I made in my thinking was based on my

experience of working with the e-commerce brands in my previous job. Not one of those brands offered a "lead magnet" to try and educate their customers about the value of their product. They simply ran marketing to their product pages and their e-commerce stores.

They got their marketing messaging right, which did 80% of the sales job for them, and they led people straight to a page where people could buy. There was no lead magnet or overcomplicated way of trying to sell products. So, my thinking was, could I apply this to digital products?

If you find yourself in this trap right of building a list of freebie hunters, let me unpack why we need to switch things up now.

The Shifting Landscape of Lead Generation

With all of the concerns that people have around their data and its use, today's consumers are savvier than ever. They're inundated with free offers and have become wary of giving away their email addresses to get something, only to then be bombarded with emails forever in order to try and get them to buy something.

It doesn't matter what niche or industry you are in. Opt-in rates for lead magnets are down across the board. Whilst they do still work to grow email lists, one of the things that you'll find is that unless you have some strategies to quickly turn that lead into a customer rather than allowing an automated email sequence to try and do that over a period of time, you are literally going to still be building lists like the old school Internet marketers of yesterday.

The greatest success that I've seen in many businesses that I've worked with over the last few years has actually been in offering low-cost products as direct offers right at the top of their funnel – exactly how e-commerce brands do it.

Back when I started the whole Internet marketing journey, we didn't have the platforms that we have today to create content, demonstrate we were an expert, and build our personal brand. Platforms like Facebook, Instagram, and TikTok just didn't exist. YouTube was in its infancy, but it was just so hard to create content because the cost of equipment and editing was just scandalous.

Now that the technology in our pocket, in the form of our smartphone, allows us to create amazing marketing content that will help position us as an expert in our niche or our industry, the task of automated email sequences once somebody has got our lead magnet, has now been passed to that public content. In essence what I'm saying is - the free line has moved.

The reason I went to town and explained my SEED

Marketing™ model in such depth is that I firmly believe that the content you produce and publish in the public domain can almost replace the need for having any free lead magnets in your funnel. I'm not saying totally replace the need for lead magnets because there are still some funnels that I have myself where I do have something for free on offer, but for real profitable lead generation, we need to do something different.

Let me put it this way... if the public content you create is now the new "lead magnet" because it does the job of building an audience of people who are interested in what you do, we need a new look at lead generation. Let me unpack for you the three pillars of profit for lead generation so that you can consider this for your own business and start to switch things up.

The Three Pillars of Profitable Lead Generation

Pillar 1 - Engaging Content

The foundation on which you will build a profitable lead generation campaign is creating content that your ideal customers want to consume.

This isn't about putting all your best content behind an

opt-in form. Instead, it's about freely sharing valuable insights that demonstrate your expertise.

Remember the SEED Marketing™ model we discussed in the last chapter? That's what you need to do to have Pillar 1 in place in your business. Let me tell you about Sarah, a client I worked with a couple of years ago.

Sarah is an Executive Coach based in Murfreesboro, Tennessee. A small city with a population of just over 165,000 people. With a specialism in helping executives and directors of companies with their own personal development, Sarah wanted to reach further than just her own town to grow our business.

She is well known in the local chamber of commerce and has served everybody from the local university through to CEOs and executives of distribution companies locally.

No matter what she tried, the content she produced and published just didn't hit the mark. It wasn't getting engagement, and the standard life coaching and personal development quotes she put out there, quoting all the gurus that everybody was looking up to, didn't really set her apart in the marketplace.

Her business only grew through her local word of mouth and face-to-face networking. It wasn't Sara's fault that her social media didn't work. That's exactly how almost every single life coach or personal development coach tries to market their business today.

After she went through my training and we worked together to reshape her marketing, she finally started to find a sweet spot where she could really engage female C-suite employees of $10m+ companies by posting engaging content related to their specific frustrations and fears.

Get the foundation of engaging content in place first, and then profitable lead generation will follow.

"Ant's program was a downright revelation for my career. I was treading water in a 5-figure pond for more years than I care to admit, but within a blink - well, two months - of working with Ant, I soared into that sweet 6-figure territory. His strategies are clear and doable, and they deliver. If you're dead set on taking your business to new heights, don't look any further. I'm aiming for 6-figures a month now, all with Ant's wise counsel, and I'm over the moon to have found a coach who's so down-to-earth, reliable, and, let me tell you, just oozing with value. The man goes above and beyond, more than you'd ever expect or he'd ever promise. Sending you the biggest hugs, Ant!"

- Sarah Greenwood
Executive Coach, Murfreesboro TN

Pillar 2 - Building an Audience

This really isn't another pillar; this is really the outcome of getting Pillar 1 in place. If you get your content marketing to a place where you get real engagement, it will build a loyal audience for you.

Audience building is now far easier for anyone. The technology previously reserved for the blue-chip companies to do their marketing is now available to us. We have access to platforms where we can build our own personal brands on a global scale. Audience building should always be our focus, before we try and start getting people onto our list.

Growing an audience is not just about growing the number of followers all the number of subscribers to your profiles that exist on the various platforms that you post on. It's far more about the level of engagement that you get, which is why if you get Pillar 1 sorted, Pillar 2 is the result of doing that well.

Responding to every comment, asking another question in reply to keep the conversation going, and encouraging the sharing of your content shows the algorithms that your content is relevant, growing your audience even more.

A little ad revenue behind some of your video posts

can also help to boost engagement, but it's not strictly needed. By targeting your specific audience with low-cost video view ads to get video views, those who don't follow you will start to see your content also. From pennies on the dollar, you can get views from 1,000's of people who didn't even know you existed. If they find your content valuable, they will stay engaged.

Be sure to focus on cultivating a following on platforms where your ideal customers already spend their time. Don't just publish on the platforms you think they are on, do some research and go to the places they are already engaging. This is going to be the best way to grow your marketing and have a funnel that converts at a highly profitable level. An engaged audience that knows, loves, and trusts you will want to take the next step.

Be insanely dedicated to building a loyal following before pitching any offers or trying to get people to opt into your latest lead magnet.

Pillar 3 - No-Brainer Direct Offers

Here's where we flip the script on traditional lead generation. When you have Pillar 1 and Pillar 2 firmly in place, then we can do something completely different from old-school lead generation strategies.

Instead of offering something for free, let's create an irresistible offer that we put in front of your audience.

Radical thinking, hey... no more "opt-in from my free thing" or begging people to register for your next free webinar – just a simple, direct, no-brainer offer to buy something from you.

- Instead of free webinars, offer paid workshops.
- For your seven-day challenge, put a ticket price on it.
- Those lead magnets that you've got take the content and create a low-cost video-based mini-course.

If you do your marketing correctly and build an audience of raving fans, direct offers will be the solution to build a list of customers instead of a list of freebie hunters.

People value what they pay for. If somebody has paid money for a product or service from you, they have attributed a level of value towards what you've offered them. And because they've paid for it, the likelihood is that they will look at it, use it, and pay attention to whatever it is that they've purchased.

If someone gets something for free, there is very little value attributed to the product that they've got access to. Most of the time, it just fills their hard drive space and collects virtual dust.

By offering a no-brainer offer instead of a free opt-in for your lead generation, you're actually building a list of customers who are choosing to buy into you. And the relationship between your list changes from having to try and convince people to buy something and always promote something on your list to providing transformational value.

The first time I implemented this...

I used to run a simple lead magnet campaign. Adverts to a landing page for people to opt-in and get a free PDF guide called "The Ultimate Funnel Blueprint" – it was building me a decent-sized list. In two months of running ads, I had grown my list by about 3,000 subscribers.

When I looked at the actual engagement stats, open rates hovered around 12%, and when I launched my $997 implementation class to this list, only 3 people bought. That's a 0.1% conversion rate.

I knew something had to change. So, I tried an experiment. Instead of giving away the blueprint for free, I turned it into a $27 "Funnel Implementation Workshop" that included the blueprint document plus a 60-minute pre-recorded online training. I gave copies of the slides and a workbook for people to download too.

In the next two months, I only added 150 people to my list - a fraction of the previous growth. But this was a good thing.

Yes, list growth dropped from 3,000 down to 150, but I went from 3 customers in the program to 150 customers just on the front-end offer. The difference in my income went from $3,000 made from chasing people via email after their opt-in to $4,050 just on the first no-brainer offer as part of the launch for my next class.

When I offered my implementation class to this smaller list of 150 people, 26 people bought it at the $997 price. That's a 17% conversion rate from a much smaller list and revenue of almost $26,000, plus the $4,050 from the workshop, meaning a total revenue of over $30,000.

This taught me two important things...

1 - People value what they pay for.

Those who invested $27 were significantly more likely to engage, implement, and ultimately invest in higher-ticket solutions. They weren't just joining a list - they were investing in a relationship with my business.

2 - Low-Cost, No-Brainer, Direct Offers Work!

Often, people fear selling on social media, directly on their ads and through their content but give people the right no-brainer offer, position it directly to them in your content marketing, and attract people who are ready to jump in. Done correctly, all of your content marketing does most of the pre-selling for you. This means that when you position your offer, you've already got people ready to take action.

A well-crafted, direct offer can do several things...

- It separates the serious prospects from the freebie hunters
- It allows customers to experience your real value firsthand
- It creates a micro-commitment, making future purchases more likely
- It distinguishes you from everybody else in your niche who is just offering free lead magnets and indirect offers

Remember, a No-Brainer Offer should provide significant value, making it an easy decision for your audience to purchase. Clearly articulating the benefits of your offer and how it will bring them transformation quicker and easier than doing it on their own is exactly why they will buy.

This kind of no-brainer, direct offer becomes even more

profitable for you when you articulate exactly what somebody is going to get when they buy from you, the timeframe it will take for them to get that, and specifically who the offer is for.

Some people, I've talked this to over the years have said that building a list of customers is slower than building a list of leads. In terms of building the number of people, yes, it is. But it's far more profitable, and big lists of freebie hunters are not always the goldmine you can bank on.

Once someone has made a purchase from you, if they get true value and a result, they will want more.

"The probability of selling to an existing customer is 60-70%, while the probability of selling to a new prospect is 5-20%"

~ from the book "Marketing Metrics" by Paul W. Farris, Neil T. Bendle, Phillip E. Pfeifer, and David J. Reibstein

Building a list of customers rather than freebie hunters is the new lead generation strategy we should all be looking to employ in our marketing. We will make money and qualify them.

Paid Lead Gen is a Qualification Process

As a final word on this paid lead generation mindset shift,

realizing that this shift in strategy does one other thing – it qualifies people to become your best clients and customers. By focusing on engaging content, building an audience, and offering no-brainer products, the leads we are generating are more highly qualified to be able to take up our main core offer or higher ticket programs.

This whole approach might result in a much smaller list, but it will be a list of people who are genuinely interested in what you offer and are willing to invest in solutions. They will be people of higher intent, ready to act and more invested in their future.

Paid lead generation campaigns that pre-qualify potential customers can speed up the sales cycle, give you higher quality clients and get you far better results from any other free lead generation activities you can have running in your business.

"The aim of marketing is to know and understand the customer so well the product or service fits him and sells itself."
~ Peter Drucker - Practice of Management

It's time for us all to move beyond the use of traditional lead magnets. We should now focus on creating engaging, high-value content, building an audience before building a list, using No-Brainer Offers to qualify leads, and then seeing things turn around for us in all of our lead-generation activities.

Remember, it's not about having the biggest list. It's about having the right list - a list of engaged, qualified prospects who are ready to buy what you're selling.

In the next chapter, we'll unpack the Minimum Viable Funnel™ framework, where we'll see how these principles of profitable lead generation fit into a streamlined, effective marketing system.

4

The Minimum Viable Funnel

Complex marketing funnels are killing businesses.

Before I closed my agency in 2023, and if I'm honest, this was probably the final straw for me, I offered a client a full refund on a project that we were working on because we were getting nowhere.

The client had bought a high-ticket program from some guru who sold it to them from the stage at an event they attended, then approached me with a specific request to build everything out. They wanted my team and I to copy the exact "blueprint" that they had been given from this $16,000 training that they bought.

We looked at the work required, quoted $19,000 to build everything out, and estimated that it would take us around

6 to 8 weeks to complete everything if we received all the content and information we needed from the client. We needed the client to produce content for the products, the funnel, and the marketing. This predominantly was focused on video content that would be used to create the entire product they wanted to launch, the videos to go on landing pages and sales pages, checkouts, upsells, and down-sells. The videos were also for use in advertising and social media.

We created and guided the client to give them a complete list of 109 videos that they needed to create and send to us. Titles of the videos, content structure for each of the videos, and specifics on things such as hooks and calls to action. It was all loaded into our task management system so that they could go through them one by one and send them our way.

Everything was in line with the "blueprint" that we were told to follow. The client was happy that we were able to simplify the implementation process for the exact framework they wanted to have in their business and that I was almost acting as a project manager for them.

But after a few weeks of chasing the client for some of this video content and answers to a number of questions that we had with regards to getting a better understanding of their product and their audience, I called time on the project. It hadn't even been a month since the client had paid us in full for this project when I offered a full refund.

The client was shocked, to say the least. However, they were completely overwhelmed with the amount of content they needed to create. It was this massive sense of overwhelm that paralyzed them from doing anything.

They were already extremely busy and very successful in their business. Still, they wanted to invest in creating this online ecosystem in a bid to transition away from the in-person consultancy work and physical workshops that they had to offer in their business.

This digital side of the business that they wanted to create would remove the challenge of needing to be away for four nights a week from home, eliminate the need to travel thousands of miles every month, and then have to spend weekends trying to catch up with business admin.

I could see this project hanging around like a bad smell for months and months and months because we were so reliant on the client creating the content they needed to build out this ecosystem.

The refund was paid in full, and I gave the client three specific things to work on before coming back to me to see how I could help. Those three specific things formed part of my thinking around creating a simpler funnel framework for any knowledge-based business. When she returned three weeks later on a Zoom call with me, she was ready to go.

We implemented the MVF into her business, and within the first three weeks, she generated over 100 paid leads and 27 paying customers of her high-ticket program. A total of $135,389. Her investment with me to create this was just $2,500.

Being on the agency side of things, here's the reality most people don't see... **complex marketing funnels are killing businesses.**

Too many entrepreneurs waste thousands of dollars on building out bloated marketing systems, paying so-called "funnel hackers" their over-priced fees, and ultimately creating a system that confuses customers instead of converting them.

It slows down the process of going to market and ultimately slows down the process of earning any money from the offers that you want to present.

And just because some hotshot guru or millennial bro-marketer has told you that their "blueprint" is the solution that is "proven" to work and grow an online business, doesn't mean that it's the only solution.

Simple funnels work. They reduce friction and make the buying cycle faster, and that is why I decided to write this book in the first place. I want to both speed up the process of you being able to go to market with the offers that will transform the lives of other people around the world, but I also want you to reduce the amount that you need to invest financially in creating these funnels.

As I've talked about plenty in this book, I've learned the hard way myself, in my own business, and with some of the clients in my previous agency. I don't want you to have to go through that same learning process.

After simplifying hundreds of marketing funnels in a similar way then I've just described and by getting my hands dirty by helping people do it, I've discovered that the most successful funnels aren't the ones with all the bells and whistles. They're the ones that strip away almost everything that doesn't directly contribute to fast conversions.

The client I just shared about continues to follow the same model, running a monthly live online workshop and continuing to make 5-figures a month in her online business. Her highest revenue from one live workshop was $38,000+.

"Ant gave me something no other marketing expert could - clarity. As a D&I consultant working with Fortune 500 executives all over the US, I'm used to solving complex problems. But when I tried to build the online part of my business based on the training I bought, I just froze up.

I paid Ant's team $19,000 to set up this complicated system. It was a big investment; I gave his team everything they needed, and it was a lot of work. When they asked for all the content to build everything out, I froze again. That's when Ant did something I never expected - he gave me back my money and instead gave me three simple steps to follow. I couldn't get a refund for the training I bought, but I realized that what Ant had given me was a way to get started online that I could build on little by little. I didn't need to do everything at once. A few weeks later, I reached out to Ant again. I didn't think he'd even take my call, but he welcomed me back with such grace. I invested much less this time to get things set up, and in just 20 days, I generated 103 leads for my paid online workshop. Then, 27 of those people invested in my coaching program. With a small ad spend, I made $135,380.

Even better, I can now say NO to so many in-person consulting jobs and offer virtual services instead because Ant showed me this simple way forward.

Looking at my calendar, I've cut my travel in half and got my weekends back with my kids. ¡Qué bendición! Ant's straightforward, high-integrity approach transformed my business. I learned that just because I had the money for something complicated doesn't

mean it was the right thing to build. Como decimos en Miami, sometimes less is more. ¡Mil gracias, Ant!

~ Maria - Founder, Inclusive Outlook LLP

What I have implemented and discovered from my own campaigns and what I helped this client with, I started to name the framework the Minimum Viable Funnel™ - MVF for short.

The MVF isn't about doing less - it's about implementing fast, testing and seeing the result, then pivoting and tweaking with an intense focus on what actually works for your audience. It doesn't need fancy features or complicated attachments. It just needs to be sharp and well-maintained.

The Four Core Elements of an MVF

The four essential components every successful funnel needs can be summarised as the following...

MVF Element 1 - Effective Traffic Sources

Your funnel needs the right visitors to generate sales. But here's where I got it wrong early in my business - I tried to be everywhere at once. I was publishing content for content's sake and trying to be on every platform. Instead, I wish I had discovered and used my SEED Marketing™

model and considered advertising to boost reach to those not following me. Traffic sources for your MVF can include...

A) Your email list, if you have one

Despite all the changes in social media and marketing platforms, your email list remains one of your most valuable assets if you have built it right, as I talked about earlier in this book. It's still the most powerful traffic source you can use, and for good reason.

"Email marketing still delivers an average ROI of $42 for every $1 spent, outperforming most other digital channels"
~ Campaign Monitor

Your own email list gives you direct access to people who've already shown interest in what you offer. Unlike social platforms, you own this channel. No algorithm changes can take it away from you. You can get in front of people and stay top of mind by simply hitting send one broadcast, not sending content out and hoping that people will see it.

B) Strategic partnerships

Getting other people to introduce you to their audience can multiply your reach without multiplying your work. Joint live webinars are especially powerful here.

Take my client, James, who runs a financial planning firm in Salt Lake City. He was struggling to break through in a crowded market. Rather than pouring money into ads that kept getting rejected every time he tried to run a campaign when we started to work together, I suggested a totally different approach.

From his list of other business contacts, we identified three complementary businesses that served the same audience but didn't compete with him directly. He approached them with a partnership proposal for co-hosted webinars. He first suggested that it would be great to have them present to his audience and then suggested a return webinar for their audience to hear from him.

After he had an accounting firm serve his audience, his first return joint webinar with the same company brought in 312 highly qualified leads - more than he could cope with! In fact, this was more leads than his previous 10 webinars combined.

Why was there such a difference? Borrowed trust. When you are recommended to someone else's audience, they're far more likely to give you a chance.

Look for partners who serve the same audience as you but solve different problems. Approach them with a proposition that benefits their audience first, not just your business.

And James... those 312 leads? We handled all the leads with a commission-only salesperson team of three people, and they sold 89 people into his Family Financial Planning program in just under two weeks. He paid the sales team a 35% commission and still banked $115,526.45 on a $1,997 offer. Not bad, really, when there was no ad spend, and he presented to someone else's audience of 90 minutes.

C) Targeted advertising

Despite sharing some non-ads strategies with you, I firmly believe ads are an amazing way to test messaging, landing pages, and content; plus, you can get in front of people who do not know who you are in a matter of minutes these days.

But ads are where many business owners go wrong - they start with large ad budgets before they have a proven funnel and end up burning through cash.

Ads can and do work with low-level budgets and are amazing at testing things. Imagine creating 3 landing pages, each with different headlines and content, then you create 3 ad campaigns and put $10 per day on each. You run this for a couple of weeks and then close the two losers and bump up the budget on the winner.

It would always be my strong advice to test ads on lower budgets for a period of up to three weeks, then only put larger budgets behind things that work. This is something a lot of ad agencies will not tell you. They want you to give them access to your credit card and will want to spend as much as they can, as fast as they can to prove their worth – and charge you a management fee for the privilege too.

Only use paid advertising when and only when the numbers make sense to do so, and always start with small budgets to make sure the ads work.

I remember working with a client who was eager to "go big" with Facebook ads right away. Instead, I convinced her to start with just $20 per day with a cost per lead of $14. For the first week, the results were disappointing - high costs and few conversions. But this small test allowed us to identify and fix what wasn't working without wasting thousands. By week three, her cost per lead had dropped to just $3.50. The funnel did the rest of the work.

Many businesses that I worked with, and many of my own ad campaigns, saw Facebook ad costs go up in 2023. This makes testing and optimization more crucial than ever. Start small and track carefully. Only scale when you have data to show that your ads are working. Remember, you might not make a profit on the front end of an ad campaign, so measuring the whole funnel is crucial to measuring your Return On Ad Spend (ROAS).

D) Content marketing

This one is easy - use the SEED Marketing™ model we covered earlier to form the foundation of a sustainable traffic source from content marketing. Long-form or short-form content, it all to drive traffic.

This isn't about posting constantly but about creating strategic content that positions you as the go-to expert in your niche. When they see you as the solution to their problems or someone who can help them achieve their ambitions and goals, they will buy when you make them the right offer.

"People don't just buy goods and services.
They buy solutions to their problems."
~ Mark Cuban

Remember, the goal isn't to drive just ANY traffic to your MVF - it's about attracting the RIGHT traffic.

Focus on one or two traffic sources initially, master them, and only expand when you're consistently seeing results.

MVF Element 2 - Free and Low-Cost Offers

Remember what I said about profitable lead generation previously? This is the part of every funnel where traditional thinking needs a complete overhaul.

Presenting your audience with a low-cost, no-brainer, direct offer and testing just one lead magnet is how I would start here.

Personally, a few years back, when I looked at what I was doing in my own marketing and funnel, I was horrified. Over the years, I have created so many "free" things that people could download and get access to. I was blogging and linking to lead magnets that would help readers understand more by choosing to opt in and download a PDF, eBook, or guide that I had written.

I went through all the blog posts, counting and trying to index them, but I lost count and gave up when I got to 48 lead magnets. Everything from guides on defining your ideal customer, creating lead magnets, writing sales pages... and so much more. Everyone could get access to pretty much all my knowledge if they downloaded everything. And for free!

When I started to re-think my strategy around lead generation and to create the MVF for myself, just after the COVID lockdowns, it was admitting to myself that I was not helping myself to build a profitable business if I was giving all this away for free – so, I removed all the links to lead magnets from my blog and did two things...

Number 1 – I focused on offering one checklist that gave direct implementable steps people could implement within 15 minutes.

Number 2 – I then positioned a low-cost, no-brainer offer on the thank you page after opt-in, and I drove traffic to the offer as well.

Instead of just funneling people onto my list and then sending a million emails to get them to buy something, I presented an offer immediately!

If you want to use a free opt-in product, like the old-school lead magnet, focus on something that can bring instant transformation in just a few minutes. It has to be high-value content that showcases your expertise and gives action steps to take. Forget all the people who say you need to give away information in free lead magnets; that's not what people want. People want TRANSFORMATION. Give it to them with a guide or checklist they can follow to take action on.

The no-brainer offer that you put immediately on the thank

you page should then help the person to do one or both of the following...

1. To get a result faster or easier than just using the free opt-in.

2. To go deeper into the subject and help them learn even more.

By doing this, you will have a direct offer in front of people immediately. This means that 100% of those who opt-in will see this offer.

Now, in my own business, I run direct traffic to a $27 training called "Selling Without Selling" as well as traffic to a free PDF sales conversation checklist that details the same offer on the thank you page.

Both ways of driving traffic to my no-brainer offer produce a profit, and every month, I check in on the stats. And further sales then come off the back of that with the next step of the MVF in place – a high-converting event that helps people to connect with me, Human to Human. I don't leave automated emails and AI bots to make that connection.

MVF Element 3 - Conversion Events

The third part of the MVF is where the sales start coming in a big way. When we have our marketing done right, traffic coming into our free opt-in products and low-cost offers, we need to connect with our customers at a human level to cultivate a real relationship with them and move them into our other products and services.

Conversion events that work today take three main forms. All of them are focused on doing the exact opposite of what most people are suggesting you do with your online marketing today. Instead of bots, AI, and full automation, the MVF brings the human back into the funnel so that the leads coming in can experience and engage with the real you in some way. I want to unpack some of the best conversion events you could use in your funnel.

Conversion Event 1 - Webinars and Live Online Workshops

During my marketing career, I have seen clients use webinars in their funnels to generate significant income. At times, webinars were outperforming anything else to make sales. Many experts and gurus still teach that webinars are the best strategy to be able to generate sales.

Personally, I've seen a couple of different ways that webinars have been used, and I think that now is the time to rethink our relationship with webinars. They are not the silver bullet that many people make them out to be.

Structuring a successful webinar presentation today totally differs from what used to work a decade ago. In my own business, and with some clients, I have seen a number of underperforming webinars and some that are absolutely crushing it. I believe that there is one type of webinar that is working best right now which many people are adopting. Let me share how one client has implemented this and the results he gained from it.

I remember starting work with one of my previous agency clients – Clive, a real estate expert in Canada. The first thing I did was switch off the advertising that he had been running for the last 6 months, sending traffic to an evergreen and automated webinar. It wasn't converting any sales.

He was following a strategy that he had learned from a webinar "expert" and spending over $1,000 on adverts every week, getting handfuls of daily registrations, then averaging a less than 10% watch rate of those who registered for the webinar. 1 or 2 people per month were completing an application to have a call with him. From those who booked a call, only 2 people showed up and no one bought in the entire 6 months.

We did the sums (or than math)...

- Six months advertising spend - $21,104
- Clicks from ads to registration page – 8,441 clicks
- Webinar registrations – 603 (7.1% conversion from click)
- Unique webinar viewers (Total) – 58 (9.6% of registrants)
- Average webinar view time – 46% of webinar
- Applications in 6 months – 9 (15.5% of registrants)
- Sales Made - $0

Clive had no tracking or reporting set up to measure the effectiveness of his webinar funnel. Let's break down the stats above and see what I suggested he do instead... and his results.

Click-Through to Registration Conversion (7.1%)

I'd expect a higher conversion rate for registrations to his webinar than this. 7.1% is very low. The landing page was not converting well. This could be a messaging mismatch between the promise made in the advertising and that on the landing page, a weak headline, poor layout, or too much friction in terms of content or scrolling to get to the registration part. On the other hand, the ad targeting could be too broad or completely off, bringing in totally the wrong people to the page.

Webinar Show-Up Rate (9.6%) & Watch Time (46%)

Evergreen, or on-demand, webinars have lower show-up rates than live ones. There's less urgency. People don't feel like they'll miss anything. They often register out of curiosity, with no commitment, expecting to see a replay available on email that they'll watch later but don't.

Live webinars typically have a show rate of anything between 20 to 40%, in my experience, with on-demand or evergreen webinars often having a less than 10% show-up rate.

My client was around this figure for show up's to watch, but most people didn't even watch all the way through to the point that he made an offer of a coaching call with an initial application.

Application Rate (9 applications - 15.5% of viewers)

This was the shining light in the funnel, but with such low volumes, statistically, it was still something that we couldn't necessarily rely on for a positive indication of something working.

15.5% of webinar viewers applied for a call with him. That's very strong. This was suggesting that his program was something that people actually were interested in wanting to apply to join. The right people, when they watch, are converting to book calls. The problem isn't the offer itself or the application page – it's getting enough people to see the offer to apply, or the system the webinar was running on was tracking viewers wrong.

We won't even unpack the fact that 7 people didn't show up for calls, and from the 2 that he spoke with, nobody bought from him.

How did we fix this?

In looking at all of these numbers, there were so many things that we could've thought about trying to implement, but I changed the angle of his delivering the presentation completely. We completely scrapped the idea of running a webinar using a template from one of the marketing "secrets" books that he was running and instead did this...

We set up a weekly, $27, live online workshop to sell his $3,500 coaching program by offering a $500 application to join his main core offering.

Yes, we canned the free webinar completely and reworked his webinar presentation to be much more of a training workshop than an empty webinar he had created using the template he'd been given to use by some webinar guru.

Plus, he made an offer at the end of every workshop, not just the ability to apply for a call. Here's the setup now...

- We changed the name from "Free Webinar" to something with a much higher perceived value... "Live Property Development Masterclass and Q&A" (that was his niche).

- Set a fixed weekly time and run it live that worked with his schedule and a time that other events typically happened in this niche (Every Wednesday at 7 pm).

- There was a charge of $27 to attend, and no replay would be provided.

- A printable PDF workbook was provided.

- The offer to work with him was a $500 application, which would be discounted from his $3,500 program – all mentioned at the end of the workshop.

- Within the first month, these were the results...

- 116 registrants from $3,700 LinkedIn advertising spend - this meant his $27 ticket price had already generated $3,132 in sales, almost breaking even on his ad spend.

- 96 people showed up – an 82.7% show-up rate. Whilst people were paying, there wasn't quite a 100% show-up rate, but within one month, we almost doubled the number of people showing up to an online workshop rather than a free webinar.

- 22 people paid $500 to complete an application to work with him in his coaching program. Every single one of these people showed up to the call with him.

- 19 people then paid a further $3,000 each to join his program. The 3 people that didn't buy.

- Total sales for his program in its first month of running this campaign – 19 sales at $3,500 = $66,500

Webinars aren't dead - it's just the way most people use them.

Let's be honest about evergreen webinars. It's 2024 as I am writing this, and as I have said a few times in this book, things are working totally differently online today than in years gone by. If you're reading this book any time into the future, I know that this could all have changed again. That's the frustrating thing about the online marketing world, things change so rapidly. This is why we need to stay on top of these things rather than just running a strategy that somebody came up with ten years ago, thinking that it won't work for us today.

The promise of evergreen or on-demand webinars sounds like a dream, but they always hide problems you can't see until you've wasted thousands on ads or months on organic marketing – or both!

The switch to a $27 live online "event" for Clive, instead of making it free, gave people the live interaction they wanted, brought real human connection, and put a value on spending the time attending.

Running it live every Wednesday at 7 pm meant that advertising could be constantly running, with a "show up" sequence of emails for those that registered to remind them to attend, plus it was just in Clive's calendar to be at his desk every Wednesday evening.

The workbook they downloaded right after purchase gave them a slight glimpse into the content and an introduction "Thank You" letter from my client; at the start of the PDF, it gave information on his background and expertise, so he didn't have to do it all on the workshop.

The no-replay message created a sense of scarcity, and I believe I was partly responsible for the show-up rate he achieved.

The $500 application fee that counted toward the program if they were accepted was just to prequalify people for the main offer.

With an 82% attendance, he generated $66,500 in program sales in just one month, and by almost breaking even on advertising, Clive got his time and confidence back. He stopped chasing clicks that went nowhere and started turning real attention into commitment and commitment into clients.

This is a total strategy shift away from what all the "bro marketers" and marketing strategists who haven't moved with the times are still telling us to do. By creating something of huge value, not just a sales opportunity, including direct offers, no hidden pricing, and a true human connection event, he made sales.

If you're thinking of using webinars or live online workshops, stop building an expensive list of freebie hunters and build a list of customers right from the start.

Conversion Event 2 - Discovery Calls

Nothing beats a real conversation. Ever since we've come out of the COVID-19 lockdowns, everybody wants to have a greater level of human connection that allows them to have real conversations and make real, genuine connections with people.

Almost every business needed to pivot online to create a sense of connection through using technology because we couldn't meet face-to-face. During that time, many of the technologically savvy marketers started to create systems and processes that would automate a lot of this connection, even using AI and bots to be able to do some of this work. I'm even seeing some marketers now suggesting they've created AI systems to do outbound telephone calls and have conversations with people to book appointments.

All of this automation, technology and use of AI is stripping away and eroding the fundamental aspect of sales that increases conversion like nothing else. **Real human connection**.

Within the coaching and online expert space, discovery calls have been the staple of many people's businesses. The mindset was that if you were able to offer somebody a 30-minute call where you could serve them, you would then be able to pitch them your product or your service. This inevitably led to many people making calls for free, and eventually, many people got wise to the fact that a discovery goal was simply a sales call dressed as something else.

There is a much better way to run discovery calls in order to be able to make more sales. We'll cover this in detail in the Selling Without Selling™ section of this book, but I want to share with you how this type of conversion event has helped me to grow my business more than any other conversion event that I could've put into my funnel.

From 2011 to 2023, I ran and operated a done-for-you marketing agency, employing people locally here in the UK to deliver work for clients. We were serving people to build their funnels and their online courses and get their business systems running well on Kajabi. In the agency's early days, people were buying because they were having lots of conversations with me. Then, as the agency started to grow, I looked at ways of systematizing the sales process and dealing with the inquiries coming into the business in a better way because I had less time.

Inquiries would come in through the website or from emails, and we picked all the elements from a menu of our services and just pasted them into a Canva document, and sent them to the client. There was very little consultancy or conversation because we would simply be responding to what the customers were asking us for. I even got things to the point that I had a level of automation set up to take inquiries through a form that would then be processed through a Google doc, and it would send a proposal to me that I could check, tweak if needed, and then send it on.

I fell into the trap of mass automation and systematization of something so important to my business that I wasn't serving my customers in the best possible or my business.

It felt like I had abdicated the responsibility for dealing with inquiries to computers and systems. At the end of 2019, I put a stop to it all.

Everything in our business became about offering services that were positioned and priced based on the value of the transformation we could bring to the potential client, not on the hours it would take to do something.

Every inquiry resulted in the customer getting on a call with me so that I could discuss with them the challenges that they were having in their business and the aspirations that they had for their business; then, I could prescribe the ideal next steps that I believe they should take in order to achieve their goals.

Sales became far more consultative, and as a result, I started to convert far more sales inquiries into paying customers. In fact, even though I don't have an agency anymore, I still operate in the same way for all of my private client sales inquiries. **It's helping me to convert 90% of sales calls.**

I've packaged together the whole process that I run for bringing inquiries into my business, triaging those inquiries, and having the right sales conversation with everyone. I call this process Selling Without Selling™, and it's part of the final element of the MVF in this book.

We all have to understand that selling is not about persuasion or manipulation anymore. That may have been how we used to get trained around sales, but today, I believe we can help people to make better buying decisions with the right type of conversation. Rather than trying to shoehorn them into buying a particular product or service through our clever sales tactics, helping to get them to the point of realization they want to buy should be our goal.

Conversion Event 3 – Sales Pages

If you're thinking about building a sales page for your funnel and product or service, then listen to me really clearly when I say that your sales page doesn't need fancy animations, clever functionality, or added plug-ins to make it convert. It needs clarity.

I built a 5,000-word sales page based on a template and framework that I was given by a very successful online business owner. His thing was, "You need all of these elements to make your sales page convert better than anybody else's" – it wasn't true, for my business anyway. After two launches with this sales page I was told to build for myself by my coach, I chose to do something completely different; instead of adding in all of the elements that I was instructed to do, with all the extra features and the copious amounts of content, conversions more than doubled on my next launch when I built a page based on the data that I had gathered from my two previous launches.

This wasn't just luck. It was a direct result of stripping away unnecessary parts of my page that didn't matter to customers, and I had evidence that some parts just didn't matter. There is a tool that I recommend people install into their website websites to see what customers are doing on their sales pages, called HotJar. It essentially screen records the activity that someone performs on your page anonymously, so you can see what parts of the page people are reading and interacting with. I removed a lot of complexity and decided to focus on what actually matters to customers.

You see, most people approach sales pages backward. They start by listing every feature, bonus, and technical detail of their product. They create endless scrolling pages filled with fancy graphics, countdown timers, and popup messages - all because some marketing guru told them more is better.

The truth is simplicity sells.

By using MVF principles that I've now packaged together as a framework to build out a sales page, I've cut down the work and the thinking that you need to do in order to create the best content for your sales page into **Five Core Elements**...

1. A clear statement of the problem your audience faces
2. Your unique solution (with social proof)
3. The transformation your customers could expect
4. Simple pricing and offer details
5. FAQ section addressing common objections

I created a nicely designed page that had a great flow of messages without any animation and certainly with no 20-minute sales video, and my next launch doubled in conversion from the previous two.

"If you can't explain it simply, you don't understand it well enough."
~ Albert Einstein

What also happened during my launch was that I had far fewer questions coming in during the launch process, trying to clarify what people were buying.

Instead of questions about my entire bonus stack and asking, "Can I just buy this one bonus on its own?" I had people saying things like, "This is exactly what I've been looking for," and "I finally understand how this works."

Your High-Converting MVF Sales Page

When it comes to sales pages, there is so much that we could talk about in terms of all the different sections that you can build out to make it highly converting. The five core elements that I mentioned a moment ago are what people need to spend more time on than any other part of their page. Here is my rundown of these five core elements.

1. A Clear Statement of the Problem

This is where you show your audience you understand their struggles. Don't rush past this part - it's the foundation of your entire sales page.

Start with a headline that speaks directly to their biggest pain point. Then, use the first section of your page to expand on this pain, showing you truly understand what they're going through.

What makes this work is specificity. Instead of saying, "Marketing is hard," say, "Spending hours creating content that nobody sees is frustrating." The more specific you are about the problem of the person reading your sales page, the more they'll trust that you can solve it.

I worked with an accountant who struggled for months

to sell her bookkeeping program. Her original sales page jumped straight into features. I rewrote just the headline to start with and used "Drowning in receipts and spreadsheets? Tired of staying up late trying to make sense of your business finances?" The result...

...sales tripled the following month with the same advertising budget that she'd had before. Clarity of the problem won the day.

2. Your Unique Solution (With Social Proof)

After addressing the problem, present your solution clearly. This isn't about listing features yet - it's about positioning your approach as the answer to their problems. It's about educating your visitors to your sales page so that you can bring about the transformation they are looking for.

What makes your solution different? Why should they choose you instead of competitors or doing nothing? This is where your unique approach matters.

Include social proof early in the form of one or two powerful testimonials that speak directly to the main problems you just outlined can be more effective than a dozen generic reviews.

My client, Daniel, included a video testimonial from a customer who said: "I was exactly where you are now - overwhelmed and ready to quit. Six weeks later, I've doubled my client base." This single testimonial outperformed pages of text about his program features.

3. The Transformation They Can Expect

This is the heart of your sales page. People don't buy products or services - they buy outcomes and transformations. Make this crystal clear.

Don't waste time just listing what they'll get (features). Focus instead on what they'll become or achieve after using your solution (benefits). Show the contrast between their current struggles and where they'll be after working with you.

Use specific examples and paint a picture of what success looks like. "Imagine opening your inbox every Monday to find 5 new client inquiries without spending a penny on ads" is far more compelling than "You'll get more leads."

Even consider creating a "Before and After" section that clearly shows the contrast between where they are now and where they'll be. This helps prospects visualize the transformation your offer delivers.

4. Simple Pricing and Offer Details

Once the visitor to your sales page understands the

transformation, you're only job then is to make your offer impossible to misunderstand.

Over the years of being in the agency world, I've seen so many sales pages offering products, services, memberships, courses and masterminds where the pricing and packages are so confusing and complicated. Clear pricing, simple packages, and a straightforward explanation of what they'll receive when they buy are what you need to present to your potential new customer.

Too much choice often leads to decision paralysis and abandoned sales pages. Offering 2-3 carefully structured choices can increase overall conversion. When you present just one offer, you create a binary decision - yes or no. The customer either buys or clicks away. But with a couple of options, you shift the decision from "Should I buy?" to "Which one should I get?" This is a psychological shift that is subtle but powerful.

The important thing to do is create meaningful differences between your options. Each should offer a clear value in terms of the transformation value at its price point, with features that make sense to your specific customer. This isn't about confusing people with endless choices; it's about giving them enough options to find their comfort zone without overwhelming them.

Keep your traffic sources focused, your lead generation simple, and the overall message of your offer clear.

When I had multiple coaching offers for my business displayed on my sales page a few years back, I was not getting many conversions on the sales page. I took down some of the options and just left visitors with two options to choose from. I moved away from having packages that gave them a free 20-minute call, 2-hour, 4-hour, and 8-hour packages, and a link to a high-end coaching and implementation package. Confusing right! That was 5 offers.

When I simplified the page and gave the offer of either one call per month or two calls per month, it went off like a rocket. The clarity made decision-making easier for people, and I was getting booked solid.

5. FAQ Section Addressing Common Objections

Every potential customer has objections before buying. Your job is to address these head-on rather than hoping they'll overcome them on their own. Think about the most common questions and concerns your customers have. Do they worry about time commitment? Technical skills needed? Is support available? Price justification? Address these directly in your FAQ section.

This isn't just helpful information - it's objection handling without feeling pushy. When you answer objections before they're even asked, you remove the final barriers to purchase.

Keep your FAQ section focused on the specific concerns that might prevent someone from buying. This isn't the place for general information about your business - it's about removing final obstacles to purchase.

What about the rest of my sales page?

As I said previously, these five core elements are parts of a sales page that need more attention than most people ever give them. There are other elements that we need to build into a high-converting sales page, but they can all be driven by the information you gather around these points.

Your sales page doesn't need to be a 50-page scroll fest full of animations, fancy graphics, and 1000 testimonials. It needs these five elements, presented clearly and authentically, then dressed with other things such as a curriculum or the main features that they're going to get in the offers. When you focus on clarity over complexity, your conversions will increase. A good MVF sales page shouldn't win design awards. It should win customers.

If you want a simple template for a sales page that actually converts, here it is...

- Headline that speaks to their pain point
- A short introduction showing you understand their problem
- Your solution and how it's different
- 2-3 specific testimonials addressing common objections
- Offer description focusing on transformation (benefits)
- Simple pricing packages (features)
- A guarantee
- FAQ section addressing remaining concerns
- Final call to action

Visit the resources page of this book for a downloadable checklist on building a high-converting MVF sales page. **Scan here >**

That's it.

You don't need more than this to start making sales.

Testing What Matters

One last thing about sales pages – test, test, and test again. All of the important elements that I've talked about that should be focused on, should be tested.

You don't need to get into the weeds of testing button colors and whether flashing numbers on your pricing matters or not; what I mean is the testing of these following things more than anything else...

- Your headline
- Your main offer
- Your price point
- Your guarantee

Just these four elements will typically account for 80% of your conversion rate. Using a platform like Kajabi, you can split-test your sales pages for these different elements. It's important that you test these things to ensure that they all resonate with your audience to improve your conversions over time.

In an MVF, your sales page should be seen as a conversion tool that can work 24/7 without requiring your direct involvement. Unlike webinars or discovery calls that demand your time, a well-crafted sales page can continuously convert visitors while you focus on other aspects of your business.

Remember, though, just like the other conversion events we've discussed, your sales page isn't a substitute for providing real value. It's simply a clear pathway for people who are ready to take the next step with you.

Conversion Event 4 – Email Nurture Sequences

An email nurture sequence is a sequence of emails that are programmed to be delivered to your target customer after they've taken a particular action. This is an automated way of communicating and adding more value after they opt-in for something for free from your website or they make a purchase.

Your nurture sequence should keep people engaged and move them naturally toward your core offer. But forget 50+ email indoctrination sequences. Focus on providing value and building genuine connections over time.

A simple yet effective nurture sequence includes the following:

- **Welcome and Orientation** - Make new subscribers feel at home and welcomed into your world. Share your best content and set clear expectations of how they can expect to get more value from you. This isn't about selling - it's about serving.

- **Value Delivery** - Provide actionable insights they can implement immediately. Show them you can help by actually helping them. Involved them in community conversations where possible to get value from being around others in your world.

- Problem Expansion - Help them to understand the full scope of their challenge and why common solutions often fail – pointing to why your solutions work.

- **Solution Presentation** - Introduce your solution as the natural next step, not a high-pressure pitch.

Getting Ready to Put Your MVF Into Action

Now that we've gone through the core elements and conversion events, it's time to roll up your sleeves and start building your own Minimum Viable Funnel™ - here's a complete checklist on exactly how to get started.

There are resources to help you with your implementation over. To get access, scan this QR code or head to: **www.simplifythefunnel.com/resources**

1. Audit Your Current Marketing Systems

Before building anything new, look hard at what you already have. Pull out a notebook and write down...

- What's working right now? (Look at actual numbers, not gut feelings)
- What traffic sources bring you qualified leads?
- Which offers convert best?
- What parts of your funnel feel overcomplicated or waste time?

This audit might feel painful, but it's necessary. I've seen clients discover they were spending thousands on tools and systems that produced zero sales.

2. Choose Your Primary Traffic Source

Focus on one or two traffic sources first. Based on your audit...

- Pick the traffic source that's already showing promising results
- Or choose the one most aligned with your strengths and audience

- Commit to mastering this source before adding others

Instead of trying to juggle five platforms, double down on one for the next three months.

3. Create One Compelling Offer

Your MVF needs a clear, simple offer that solves a specific problem...

- Focus on creating either a low-cost direct offer ($27-$97) or a high-value free opt-in
- Make sure it delivers real transformation rather than just providing information
- Create a simple sales conversion event
- Remove unnecessary bonuses, complicated pricing tiers, and content that adds friction

4. Build a Simple Nurture Sequence

Don't create 50 emails. Start with these four key messages...

- **Welcome -** Make them feel valued and explain what to expect
- **Value -** Provide something immediately useful related to their opt-in

- **Problem** - Expand on why their challenge is significant
- **Solution** - Present your core offer as the logical next step

Keep each email focused on one main idea.

5. Test, Measure, and Optimize

The MVF isn't "set and forget" – it's about quick implementation, testing, and improvement...

- Track key metrics for each step (traffic, opt-ins, sales)
- Test one element at a time (headlines, offers, prices)
- Pay attention to customer questions and objections
- Make adjustments based on data, not opinions

6. Add Human Connection

Remember, technology is just a tool – people buy from people...

- Schedule time for personal outreach and connection
- Follow up personally with your most engaged prospects
- Consider adding a live element (Q&A sessions or live online workshops)

- Never fully automate the relationship-building part of your funnel

7. Scale What Works

Only after you have a profitable, functioning MVF, it's only then you should you think about scaling…

- Increase budgets on traffic sources that deliver results
- Consider adding a second traffic source
- Add additional offers only after your core offer is converting well
- Maintain the MVF mindset – simplicity scales better than complexity

In the next chapter, we'll jump into my Selling Without Selling™ framework – a conversational approach that helps you convert prospects without feeling pushy or manipulative. This is how you'll turn your MVF traffic into loyal, high-value customers.

Remember, there are resources, templates, swipe files and more to help you implement as much of this as you can. Scan this QR code or visit...

www.simplifythefunnel.com/resources

5

Selling Without Selling™

Scan here to access the complete Selling Without Selling™ video training with immediate access

WWW.SIMPLIFYTHEFUNNEL.COM

The Art of Authentic Engagement

Let me start by saying I could've written an entire book on this one chapter. But I want to give you the entire framework without any fluff and the waffle so that you can implement it right away in addition to your MVF.

It's my own personal experience, and the experience of many people who become clients and part of my community, that the current business world is full of sales techniques that feel pushy, automated, impersonal and completely inauthentic.

When I completed my coaching accreditation and certification to become a Mastercoach, there was a lightbulb that went on in my mind.

I had come from a world of sales, having worked in the property world and a couple of other industries, that required me to focus on sales. I had been trained in very traditional sales techniques. Becoming a coach gave me a different way to consider thinking about sales, and in 2016 when I completed my certification, I changed everything that I did in terms of how I sold my services.

Selling Without Selling™ became the framework that I stuck to and the method by which I trained team members and clients to help them sell more of their products and services. Essentially, it's a method that transforms the way we view sales, focusing on serving the customer and providing real value in a consultative way.

I remember that it was during my five-day final coaching accreditation week when I was a resident with a number of other coaches going through the same process, and I was having coffee with one of them during the afternoon break. They were asking specifically about how to market and sell their coaching services.

The accreditation week that we were on was only focused on helping us with our coaching skills and not business development. Practicing a coaching conversation framework that we had gone through that week, I actually turned it into a sales conversation without thinking about it.

By the end of the coffee break, I had a new client, and I hadn't tried to sell anything in the way that I was trained to sell. What I did was help that person realize that they ultimately wanted to buy from me. This was when the philosophy behind Selling Without Selling™ was born.

At its core, Selling Without Selling™ is about shifting the focus from closing deals to solving problems and building relationships.

It's not about persuasion or manipulation. It's about helping potential customers realize the benefits of your product or service on their own terms and then getting to the point of realization they want to buy.

Coaching is the art of helping somebody to get to the point of realization that change needs to happen. This is why it dovetailed so well into having sales conversations.

If I could help somebody, by asking them the right questions, get to the point of realization that my product or service was perfect for them to be able to achieve the transformation they want, they would ask me to buy and I wouldn't need to sell.

"People don't buy for logical reasons.
They buy for emotional reasons."
~ Zig Ziglar, sales expert and motivational speaker

The Complete 7-Part Selling Without Selling™ Framework

You've got towards the end of this book, and I now want to give you the secret sauce. Few people will get to this part of the book, or they might have skipped to it and missed everything else that you've already read.

My aim is to serve you and give you a conversational framework that you can have in all of your sales conversations moving forward and that you can build into things that we've talked about in this book around sales pages and email sequences.

If you use this framework in the correct way, you can improve your video sales letters, your webinars, your public speaking keynotes, your sales pages and your email sequences.

Think about the following 7-step framework as a conversation where you ask questions and simply have a conversation with your potential customers to help them get to the point of making a buying decision. At times, you may need to ask more clarification questions, but if you stick to this process, you'll be able to move forward and have more success in your sales conversations. Since 2016 when I implemented this into my business and my sales process, I'm converting around 90% of the sales calls that I have with people. I want the same for you.

Step 1 – Ask, "What's Bugging You Right Now?"

This first question is designed to uncover the real pain points and challenges your potential customer is facing.

Too many sales conversations start with the salesperson talking about their product features or company history. Instead, give your prospect the floor. The number one thing that people love to talk about more than anything else is themselves. And you're allowing them to do that.

The important word in this question is **"now"** - you want to understand what's causing them immediate frustration or pain. This focuses the conversation on their current situation rather than hypothetical problems in the future. You want to know what is going on in their life or in their business right now.

You can phrase this question in different ways, and you should. Your own language patterns and industry, the country that you live in, are all going to be different from mine, but the essence of this question must always remain the same - to discover the pain that they have now.

Examples of how you could rephrase this could be...

- "What's the biggest challenge you're facing in your business right now?"
- "What's critical for you to resolve at this moment?"
- "What's the one thing that's keeping you up at night?"

Listen carefully to their response. Often, what they say first is just the surface issue. Ask clarifying questions to go deeper, like "Why is that a problem?" or "How is that affecting you?" These follow-up questions help reveal the true pain points.

As said, people love talking about themselves and their challenges. Your job at this stage is to listen more than you speak. Take notes if needed, or use an AI transcription tool to do this job for you, but be fully present, give your undivided attention, and show genuine interest in understanding their situation. This builds trust and shows you care about their specific issues, not just making a sale.

This question serves another important purpose - it helps you to start to understand and determine if your solution is actually going to be a good fit for their problem. If it's not, you can cut a conversation really short, suggest something else, or even refer them to someone who can better help them. This integrity builds long-term trust and reputation. You waste less of your time and less of theirs.

Step 2 – Ask, "What's Going to Happen if You Don't Get That Sorted?"

Once you understand their current challenges, this next question helps them unpack for you and explore the consequences of not solving their problem. It brings clarity to both of you about what's at stake.

This step is crucial because it helps your prospect visualize the negative future they want to avoid. It taps into the powerful human motivation to avoid pain and loss. The move away from pain is a greater motivator than a move towards pleasure. And when people clearly see the cost of inaction, they become more motivated to find a solution. There are three key benefits for asking this question second in a sales conversation...

1. It helps your prospect internalize the true cost of not finding a solution to their problem

2. It creates urgency without you having to manufacture it

3. It gives you valuable information about what they're most concerned about losing or missing

As they answer, listen for **emotional cues** as well as the practical consequences they will share with you. People often decide based on emotion and justify with logic. If they mention feeling frustrated, overwhelmed, or worried, make note of these emotional drivers.

Don't rush this step. Sometimes, the first answer they give is surface-level. Follow up with something like "And what would that mean for you?" to uncover deeper implications. The more clearly they articulate what's at stake, the more motivated they'll be to find a solution.

This question also helps you gauge how serious they are about solving the problem. If they don't see significant consequences to inaction, they may not be ready to buy. On the other hand, if they articulate clear and serious consequences, they're likely to be more receptive to your solution.

Remember that your goal here isn't to scare them but to help them clearly evaluate their situation. Be supportive and empathetic throughout this conversation.

Step 3 – Ask, "Where Do You Want to Be in X Period of Time?"

This question shifts the conversation from problems to possibilities. We've taken them down a potential rabbit hole of fear with the last question, and we want to get them out of that as quickly as possible.

More importantly, we've dug into topics of pain and fear,

so we don't want to leave them in that pit of despair. That could be seen as manipulation. We need to lift them out.

After exploring what they're trying to move away from, now you want them to describe what they're moving toward. This creates a vision of success that can be powerfully motivating.

The timeframe you choose should align with how long your solution typically takes to show results. For most services and products, 90 days is a good timeframe - it's long enough to see significant progress but short enough to feel tangible and urgent. For longer-term programs or more complex transformations, you might ask about where they want to be in 6-12 months.

Here are another few examples of how you could phrase this question...

- "What would your business look like three months from now if this problem was solved?"
- "Where would you want your health to be by the end of the quarter if we addressed these issues?"
- "What would success look like for you by Christmas?"

When we're asking them to unpack their aspirations or the transformation they want, it helps them to box in their goals and find them. This gives you clear information about what success means to them and creates positive emotional energy in the conversation after discussing the pain points you have previously.

This question also enables your potential customer to describe to you what your solution is going to be measured against in their own mind. Listen carefully to what they describe. The specifics of their desired future will tell you exactly what benefits of your solution to emphasize. If they talk about wanting more time with family, say how your solution saves time. If they mention increasing revenue, focus on the financial impact of your offer.

Sometimes, people have limited beliefs about what's possible. You can gently ask things like "What if you could achieve even more than that?" or "Have you considered the impact on [another area of their business/life]?" to expand their thinking and stretch the goals they have.

By the end of this question, you should have a clear picture of their current problems (Step 1), what will happen if they don't solve those problems (Step 2), and where they want to be instead (Step 3),

Now, you have everything you need to position your solution in the next step.

Step 4 – Ask, "OK... I Think There's a Way I Can Help... Want to Hear It?"

This simple transition question is more powerful than it might first appear. I remember, in so many sales conversations that I would have with people, the transition from "fact-finding" to "pitching" was the hardest transition. It felt like such a gear change.

By asking permission to share your solution, you put the prospect in control of the conversation. This small shift changes everything about how your offer is received.

When you say, "I think there's a way I can help," you're positioning yourself as a problem solver, not a salesperson. You're offering assistance based on what you've learned about their specific situation. This feels collaborative rather than pushy.

The key is to pause after asking this question and wait for their response. Don't rush ahead with your solution. Let them invite you to share it. When they say "yes" (and they almost always will after the previous steps), they're psychologically more open to hearing what you have to say.

The way you ask this question matters too. Your tone should be thoughtful and considerate as if you've been carefully reflecting on their situation. Avoid sounding overly confident or like you had your solution prepared before hearing their problems. This can come across as arrogant.

If they happen to say "no" or seem hesitant, this is valuable feedback. It might mean you haven't fully understood their problem, or they don't believe a solution is possible. In this case, go back to asking more questions about their situation before trying to present a solution.

When they do say "yes," you've received permission to share your solution in a way that they're ready to hear. This creates a dramatically different dynamic than launching into a pitch without being invited to do so. You will find this transition so easy. No more crunching gear changes in the conversion.

Remember, you're not selling - you're helping, and they've just asked you to help them. This mindset shift is crucial for both you and your prospect.

Step 5 – Prescribe the Ideal Next Step, and Do Not Mention Money Yet

Now that you have permission to present your solution, it's time to prescribe the ideal next step. Think of yourself as a doctor recommending a course of treatment based on a careful diagnosis. You're not selling a product - you're prescribing a solution to their specific problem.

This is where your expertise really shines. Based on everything you've learned from your conversation in steps 1-3, you'll recommend the specific product, service, or package that best addresses their unique situation. Focus entirely on the transformation it will create for them.

Here's how to structure this step effectively if I were to sell training on helping somebody simplify their marketing...

1. First, clearly state what you recommend as their next step. Be specific and confident in your prescription. For example... "Based on what you've shared, I think our 90-day implementation program would be the perfect next step for you."

2. Then, explain exactly how this solution addresses the specific challenges they mentioned in Step 1. Connect the dots explicitly... "This will directly address the conversion issues you mentioned by implementing a streamlined funnel that..."

3. Next, show how it helps them avoid the negative consequences they described in Step 2. "This means you won't have to worry about missing your quarterly revenue targets or feeling overwhelmed by tech issues."

4. Finally, describe how it will help them achieve the future state they outlined in Step 3. "By the end of the 90 days, you'll have exactly what you described - a fully functional system that generates leads while you sleep."

Throughout this explanation, I have focussed entirely on the transformation and results, not the features. I didn't say, "You'll get 6 modules and 3 Q&A calls."

What you don't do here in step 5 is just as important as what you do. And one of those don'ts...

Don't mention the price yet.

If they ask about the price immediately, gently defer with a phrase like... "I want to make sure this is the right fit for you before we discuss investment. Would you like me to explain more about how it works?"

Your goal in this step is to get them nodding along, seeing how your solution perfectly addresses their specific situation. You want them to be thinking, "This is exactly what I need" before price ever enters the conversation.

Remember, what you're doing here is prescribing, not pitching. Your recommendation should feel like thoughtful, expert advice tailored specifically to their situation - because that's exactly what it is.

Step 6 – Ask, "How Does That Sound?"

After prescribing your solution, this simple question invites feedback and confirms alignment before discussing the price. It's a crucial step that many salespeople skip, rushing straight to pricing and closing.

By asking, "How does that sound?" you're checking that they see the value in your solution and giving them space to voice any concerns or questions. This will help create a natural opening to handle objections before they become barriers. And getting another "yes" or confirmation before moving to price here helps to transition to that point.

Listen carefully to their response. Their answer will tell you exactly where you stand.

If they respond positively with comments like "That sounds perfect" or "I think that would work well," they're ready for the final step. They've essentially pre-approved your solution before hearing the price.

If they seem hesitant or have questions, this is your opportunity to address concerns before moving forward. **Don't see objections as obstacles - see them as requests for more information**. For example, if they say, "I'm not sure I'd have time for that," you can address the time commitment specifically.

If they outright object with something like "I don't think that would work for me," you need to go back to Step 5 and either clarify your solution or propose an alternative that better meets their needs.

Everything here is about creating a natural conversation flow that you may circle back on rather than a scripted sales pitch that you get stuck on when things don't go as the script has predicted it would - it very often never does.

When you step back into previous questions, You're checking in, making sure you're on the same page, and adjusting as needed. This builds huge amounts of trust because you will be seen as someone who genuinely seeks their opinion before discussing money. You demonstrate that you care more about finding the right solution than making a sale. This alone sets you apart from most salespeople.

If you receive a positive response at this stage, you've essentially received permission to discuss the price. They've agreed your solution is a good fit, which changes the entire dynamic of the pricing conversation that follows.

Remember to maintain a collaborative tone here. You're working with them to find the right solution, not trying to convince them to buy something they're uncertain about.

Step 7 – Say, "It Will Be [Cost] and Will Take X Amount of Time... How Would You Like to Pay?"

Now, it's time to discuss the investment. Having followed the previous steps properly, this final step should feel like a natural conclusion rather than a high-pressure moment.

The key is to present the price confidently and matter-of-factly without apologizing or hesitating. Your tone should convey that the value has already been established, and now you're simply handling the logistics.

Breaking this final step down into two components...

- Start by clearly stating the investment and timeframe. For example, "The investment for this program is $1,997, and we'll work together for 90 days." Be direct and specific.
- Then, without pausing, ask how they'd like to pay. "How would you like to handle the payment today?"

So, I would take a deep breath and in one sentence say... "The investment for this program is $1,997, and we'll work together for 90 days. How would you like to handle the payment today?"

This direct transition assumes the sale rather than asking for it. You're not saying, "Would you like to buy?" but rather, "How would you like to pay?" This subtle difference dramatically increases conversion rates.

This whole approach doesn't include complicated closing techniques. There are no manipulation tactics, artificial urgency doesn't rear its ugly head, and high-pressure pushes are non-existent.

The simplicity of this conversational framework is what makes it powerful.

- You've established the **true value of your solution**.
- You've linked it to their **specific problems and goals**.
- You've received confirmation that your **solution sounds good to them**.
- You've **built trust** through the entire process.

If they raise objections at this point, don't panic. Calmly address their concerns while maintaining your confidence in the value of your solution. For price objections specifically, avoid discounting immediately and think about offering...

- Payment plans
- Adjusting the package components
- Highlighting the return on investment

- Emphasizing the cost of not taking action

Remember that offering payment options can make your solution more accessible without reducing its perceived value. For example: "The full investment is $1,997, or we can break that into three monthly payments of $697 if that works better for you."

Finally, after they've indicated how they'd like to pay, guide them through the next steps. Let them know exactly what happens after payment when you'll begin working together, and what they can expect. This creates certainty and reduces any post-purchase anxiety.

Making High-Ticket Priced Offers

When it comes to pricing and payment options for high-ticket items this one breath statement here in step 7 is magic.

Currently, my coaching for private client is $60,000 for 12 months. If this is the ideal step for the person I am speaking with, I would arrive at step 7 ready to say...

"It's $60,000 to work with me one-on-one over the next 12 month as your personal CMO. How would you like to pay?"

Almost every time, there is one question that comes back

at me. "Can I pay monthly?" to which my answer is...

"Yes, for the 12-month instalment plan it's $5,000 per month."

But, I add a sweetener here. I finish by saying...

"...or you can pay in advance for the year and I will drop it to $50,000 as a single bank transfer payment."

What I have done here is use a reverse pricing mechanism.

- I gave the full price - $60,000
- For the instalments I evenly divided the price for an instalment plan - $5,000 x 12 months (the same total price)
- Then I discounted the full price if paid in advance - Saving $10,000 by paying 1 x payment of $50,000

This goes against the norms of increasing the final price if they pay in instalments. Most instalment packages make people end up paying more. Here I am rewarding action, and this is want most people end up paying to work with me.

That's Selling Without Selling™

This seven-step framework works because it follows the

natural way people make buying decisions. It starts with their problems, explores the consequences, envisions a better future, and then presents a solution - all before discussing price. By the time you reach Step 7, the value has been firmly established in your mind.

The beauty of this approach is that it creates a win-win situation. Your prospect gets a solution tailored to their specific needs, and you make a sale without resorting to pushy tactics that damage trust and reputation.

Scan to access a 5-Part video training on the complete Selling Without Selling™ framework. It's also linked from the resources page for this book at...

www.simplifythefunnel.com/resources

This framework isn't a rigid script to be followed word-for-word. If you've been given scripts from sales training programs that you've been on before, I urge you to just put them to one side or even burn them. When you follow a script, it's all two robotic, and you're not responding to the other person or the conversation that you're having. This framework allows you to do that.

Adapt the language and examples that I've given you to your personal style and niche.

What matters most is maintaining the structure and

intention of each step, not the exact phrasing. When you make it your own, it becomes more natural and effective.

Embracing Empathy and Authenticity

One of the key principles of Selling Without Selling™ is empathy - truly understanding your customer's perspective. You don't just ask about their challenges to set up your pitch; you genuinely want to understand their situation so you can help them effectively.

According to a study by PwC, **59% of all consumers feel companies have lost touch with the human element of customer experience**. This disconnect creates a massive opportunity for business owners who bring authenticity to their sales process.

Authenticity isn't just a buzzword, it's about being genuine in your desire to help. This means sometimes telling prospects that your solution isn't right for them or recommending a different approach than what you initially thought is the right thing to do rather than trying to shoehorn them into your products and services. This builds trust, and while you might not have converted a sale today, you'll gain a supporter who may become a customer later or refer others to you.

Your values should guide your sales process...

- If you value honesty, then be completely transparent about what your offering can and can't do.
- If you value education, focus on helping prospects truly understand their options.

When your sales approach aligns with your core values, it feels natural rather than forced.

This approach transforms the traditional sales process, where you're trying to "overcome objections" and "close the deal", into a collaborative process where you and your prospect are on the same side, working together to determine if your solution is the right fit for their needs.

Handling Objections With Confidence

Objections are a natural part of any sales conversation. Rather than seeing them as obstacles, view them as opportunities to provide clarity and build trust - as I said previously, they are opportunities to provide more information.

When faced with objections, follow these steps to make this part of any conversation easier.

1. **Listen Carefully** - Allow the customer to express their concerns fully. Don't interrupt or immediately jump to counter their objection.

2. **Acknowledge Their Perspective** - Show understanding with responses like "I can see why that would be a concern" or "That's a fair point." This validation makes them feel heard.

3. **Ask Clarifying Questions** - Often, the stated objection isn't the real issue. Questions like "Can you tell me more about that concern?" help uncover the true objection.

4. **Provide Context** - Once you understand the real concern, offer additional information that addresses it directly. This isn't about convincing them they're wrong but offering a different perspective.

5. **Check Understanding** - After addressing the objection, ask if your response makes sense or if they have further questions. This ensures you've resolved their concern before moving forward.

In all my time selling marketing services and training, there have been three big objections that have always come up...

- **Price** - When someone objects to price, it's rarely about the number itself. It's usually about the perceived value of transformation – either the level of result or the speed of getting the result they want. Rather than dropping your price, focus on increasing the perceived value by revisiting the transformation process that your solution provides. You may find that they're looking for a bigger result or a faster result, which could mean you could increase your price.

- **Timing** - If someone says, "Now isn't the right time," explore what would make it the right time. Often, this objection masks deeper concerns about risk or urgency.

- **Need for Consultation** - When people say they need to "think about it" or "talk to their partner/team," it usually means you haven't fully established the value or addressed a hidden concern. Ask what specific aspects they need to consider. Something absolutely golden happens when you also invite them to bring their partner or team member onto the call if it's something they need to discuss with them.

Remember that objection handling isn't about winning an argument - it's about continuing the conversation to find the right solution.

Sometimes, the right answer is that your offering isn't the best fit for them right now, and that's okay.

The Importance of Follow-Up

The sales process rarely ends after a single conversation. Effective follow-up is essential for building relationships and demonstrating your commitment to helping prospects succeed.

Follow-up should continue the consultative approach established in your initial conversation. Each touchpoint should provide additional value rather than just asking, "Are you ready to buy yet?"

Effective follow-up strategies but I've used over my time of running my business include...

1. **Value-Added Outreach** - Send relevant resources, articles, or insights that address the specific challenges discussed in your conversation. This demonstrates your ongoing commitment to helping them, whether they buy or not.

2. **Personalized Communication** - Reference specific details from your previous conversations to show you remember them and their situation. Generic follow-up messages feel automated and impersonal.

3. **Respect Their Timeline** - Be persistent without being pushy. Space your follow-ups appropriately -

immediate daily messages feel desperate while waiting too long loses momentum.

4. **Clear Next Steps** - Always end each follow-up with a specific next step or action item, whether it's scheduling another call, reviewing a proposal, or making a decision by a certain date.

5. **Shall I Delete This?** – Sending an email or a message asking whether you should delete the conversation or whether it's something they want to continue having with you will often close the deal for you. I've done this over text messages before and closed people in the follow-up. People don't like the idea of things being deleted.

"The fortune is in the follow-up."
~ Jim Rohn

Integrating Selling Without Selling™ into Your MVF

Now that you understand the Selling Without Selling™ framework let's talk about how to integrate it with the Minimum Viable Funnel™ we discussed earlier in the book.

This framework doesn't just apply to one-on-one sales calls. You can incorporate these same principles throughout your marketing funnel.

In Your Content Creation (SEED Marketing™)

Use the same questions from the framework to guide your content. Create articles, videos, or podcasts that address your audience's pain points, the consequences of those problems, and their desired future.

In Your Landing Page

Structure your copy around the same framework. Start with the pain points, address the consequences of inaction, paint a picture of what's possible, and then present your solution as the bridge between their current reality and desired future.

In Your Webinars or Presentations

Follow the same flow in your presentations. Start by discussing common challenges your audience faces (even polling them to confirm), explore the consequences, help them envision a better future, and then present your solution.

In Your Email Sequences

Each email can address a different step in the framework. Early emails focus on pain points and consequences, middle emails on the desired future state, and later emails on your solution and invitation to take action.

The New Art of Selling is Conversation.

By aligning all your marketing with this same conversational framework, you create a consistent experience for prospects no matter how they interact with your business. This builds trust and makes the eventual sales conversation feel like a natural continuation of a relationship that's already been developing.

Remember that Selling Without Selling™ is more than just a technique - it's a mindset shift that puts serving the customer at the center of your sales process. When you truly focus on helping people solve their problems, sales become the natural by-product of providing value.

6

Scaling Your Success

"The art of scaling is the art of doing the same things you've always done, just for more people."

~ Reid Hoffman, co-founder of LinkedIn

Congratulations! If you've got this far, you've learned what you need to create your Minimum Viable Funnel™. I hope you're ready to see better results from your marketing and sales processes and enjoy the rewards of simplification.

Once you've simplified your funnel, the journey doesn't end. I've given you the foundations to go to market, generate profitable leads, and win new business in a simpler, more human way. We've blended some automation with a personal connection and have brought the human back into the funnel to build relationships from the moment someone sees your content until they get the results they want.

In this final chapter, I want to explore how to scale your success and adapt your MVF as your business grows.

The Scalability of Simplicity

One beautiful thing about the MVF is its scalability. These principles work just as well for a solopreneur as they do for larger companies.

> ***"The art of scaling is the art of doing the same things you've always done, just for more people."***
> ***~ Reid Hoffman, co-founder of LinkedIn***

Let's explore how to scale each component of your MVF:

1. Scaling Your Traffic

As your business grows, you'll want to expand your traffic sources without overcomplicating things. Here are some suggestions on how you can do this.

Focus on What's Already Working

Before adding new traffic sources, maximize what's already working. If Instagram is bringing you qualified leads, increase your content there to see if this has any impact before jumping to a new platform.

Sarah, a client who teaches online art classes, was tempted to launch on three new platforms simultaneously because someone at a women's business breakfast sold her on the idea. Before she started working with this social media marketer, we first doubled down on her successful Instagram presence. She increased her frequency of posting and added more videos and carousels. Her audience grew from 3,200 to 12,000 in four months, and sales increased by 67% - all without adding complexity, just a couple more posts per week. She didn't sign with the agency that pitched her at the breakfast meeting.

Add One New Traffic Source at a Time

When you're ready to expand, add just one new traffic source and give it three months of consistent effort before evaluating. This prevents the scattered approach that burns money and energy.

As a rule of thumb I always suggest that you should only add a new traffic source when your current ones are consistently delivering results.

Start Small with Paid Advertising

Many business owners I work with fear ads because they've heard horror stories about wasted budgets or they have seen presentations from bro marketers who are telling them to spend thousands every day. Success in ads comes from starting small and being methodical.

Begin with just $10-$20 per day to test your messaging and targeting. I've seen clients get customers for their $27 products for as little as $2-3 each with this approach. Only scale up when you have proof your ads convert.

Leverage Others' Audiences Through Partnerships

One of the fastest ways to scale traffic without increasing complexity is through strategic partnerships. Look for businesses serving the same audience but offering complementary services. A joint webinar, podcast interview, or newsletter swap can instantly put you in front of hundreds or thousands of new prospects.

This approach costs nothing but time and often converts better than cold traffic because you're borrowing trust.

2. Scaling Your Offers

While keeping your core offer intact, you can thoughtfully expand your product line with additional offers that bring more customers into your ecosystem without compromising your core offers.

The Product Ladder Approach

Think of your offers as a ladder customers can climb...

- **Bottom rung** - No-brainer offers ($27-$97) that convert cold traffic

- **Middle rungs** - Core offers ($200-$1,000) that deliver your main solution

- **Top rungs** - Premium offers ($2,000-$10,000+) for those wanting more support/results

Making each offer a natural next step from the previous one is how this works best. Your $27 workshop should naturally lead to your $497 course, which should set people up for your $2,000 coaching program.

Test Before You Build

The biggest mistake I see is entrepreneurs building complex offers nobody wants. Before creating anything new, test to see if it will sell first. Some people will often suggest that you "sell it before you create it", but this is **not** what I'm saying here. I followed this strategy a number of times over the last 10 years or so, selling something before I created it.

Some clients that I worked with did this too, and they experienced the same thing I did - **It created more problems for me rather than give me any kind of helpful result.**

I was running a very busy agency at the time, and I was trying to manage that and develop training and coaching programs.

I remember doing one launch for a program, and after I sold it and the launch had closed, I had two weeks to create the first part of the training. Because of the busyness of life and the other part of my business needing all my attention, I was up until 3 am the day that it was supposed to be released, still editing the video for it. Maybe this was my unorganized and completely chaotic lifestyle that was causing this problem, but the other six modules all felt like it was a chore for me rather than something I really enjoyed doing. I vowed never to do it ever again.

When I say before you create anything new, test to see if it will sell first, I'm talking about creating a simple way to test interest without the pressure of delivery deadlines.

Create a simple sales page that describes your idea and asks people to join a waitlist or "register their interest." Or create a basic webinar that outlines the concept and gauges audience questions and engagement. You might even consider offering a single pilot module at a reduced price to see if people bite.

Maria, who teaches Spanish online, tested a new intensive program concept with a landing page that collected email addresses from interested students. When over 200 people signed up for her waitlist in a week, she knew it was worth developing - but on her timeline, not theirs. Had interest been low, she would have simply pivoted to a different concept without wasting months creating something nobody wanted.

The goal is to get meaningful feedback before investing significant time and energy. This approach gives you validation without the stress of selling something that doesn't exist yet.

Consider Adding in a Subscription Model

If you are looking for more predictable revenue, subscriptions, or memberships, help to turn one-time purchases into ongoing subscriptions. A simple $27/month membership can create stability that allows you to reinvest in growth. Just make sure the recurring value is obvious to members.

3. Scaling Your Conversion Events

As you grow, you'll need to adapt how you convert prospects into customers. There are so many different ways in which we can scale our conversion events, but there are three main ways that I really want to share with you here that have helped me personally in my business.

Balancing Automation and Personal Touch

The trick to scaling conversion events is finding the right balance between automation and human connection. Take webinars, for instance. You might start with weekly live webinars. As demand grows, you could add one of the following...

- Have a recorded version for those who can't attend live
- Ask a trained team member to host some live sessions
- Use automated webinars for basic education, saving your live sessions for Q&A and closing

The important thing is to maintain the human element even as you automate. An automated webinar that includes personal follow-up from a team member often outperforms a fully automated approach.

I feel very strongly about this, but please, never fully automate a webinar that offers you a simulated chat window, helping you to pretend that it's live. I've seen so many people get caught out by this.

In my view, if somebody is trying to trick a customer into something by pretending that you are alive when you are not, is this genuinely acting from the point of openness, trust, and with the highest level of integrity?

From One-to-One to One-to-Many

If you're currently doing one-on-one sales calls, look for ways to serve more people without losing effectiveness. Small group sales calls (3-5 prospects at once), sales webinars for larger groups, and even video sales letters with personal follow-up can work wonders.

I remember chatting with a fitness coach from Germany a few years back who was spending 13+ hours weekly on sales calls. He was following a strategy from a guy suggesting he run YouTube ads to a non-sales based webinar, just an invitation for a call. He was getting booked solid. It was burning him out.

From a 15-minute inquiry call with me, I suggested he turn this into a weekly live webinar not the evergreen one he was running, then do a group presentation at the end and pitch. For the follow up I suggested using a single, automated text message. His conversion rate stayed nearly the same, but he cut his time spent on sales calls down to 2 hours a week!

Just because someone who says that are making millions with one strategy, does not mean that it is right or that it will work for your business.

Creating a Simple Sales Team

Many small business owners think hiring salespeople is too complex or expensive. It doesn't have to be. Start with a single person who can handle initial qualification calls, even part-time. This frees you to focus only on highly qualified prospects.

Commission-based arrangements can make this affordable even for small businesses. I've seen clients successfully use 25-30% commission structures to add salespeople with no upfront cost.

4. Scaling Your Team

At some point, continued growth will require building a team - and it does not have to be a large team. What I would say is that you should never hire for every position at once. Identify your biggest bottleneck and address it first.

Often, the first hire should be someone to handle administrative tasks that pull you away from revenue-generating activities. A virtual assistant working 10-15 hours weekly can transform your productivity.

Before handing off any task, create a simple process document. This doesn't need to be complex - a bullet-point list or screen recording works fine. Some would call this a "Standard Operating Procedure" (SOP) document. This makes training easier and ensures consistency as your team grows, as others will be able to pick up this document and run with it. The secret to a good SOP is to create something that somebody of average intelligence could follow on a bad day to execute a task.

For many growing businesses, contractors make more sense than full-time hires. They reduce risk and allow you to test working relationships before making bigger commitments.

Everything from social media management, graphic design, managing your inbox, and other tasks in your business that don't require your level of genius can be outsourced and should be outsourced when it's ready for you to start handing those things over to people.

Maintaining the MVF Mindset as You Grow

As your business expands, it's easy to drift back toward complexity. You'll see the offers for new systems and widgets that you could add to your funnel. No doubt, you'll attend some business event where you get pitched from the stage on a brand-new strategy. You'll be targeted with advertising for somebody's "Proven method" to generate more sales. **Blinker yourself and guard your MVF mindset to get it working before you think about adding anything else in.**

Here are practical ways to keep the MVF mindset...

Regular Simplicity Audits

Every 90-days, review your funnel and ask..

- Is every step necessary?
- Are we collecting data we never use?
- Have we added tools that overlap with existing ones?
- Are there processes we could streamline?

I remember a time when I was paying for three different video editing software because different team members had signed up for them at different times. A simple audit saved me $2,400 annually!

Listen to Your Customers

As businesses grow, they often lose touch with their customers because they have so many. Make it a habit to read customer support emails, jump on calls with customers for feedback sessions, and review all feedback (positive and negative) that you receive.

This keeps you connected to what matters and prevents adding unnecessary complications.

Reject and Resist Shiny Object Syndrome

The marketing world constantly introduces new platforms, tools, and tactics. Most are distractions. I have made it a rule to ask the following four questions before I buy anything new...

1. Does this solve a real problem I'm having?
2. Can I achieve the same result with the tools I already use?
3. Will this genuinely improve the customer experience?
4. Do I have the capacity to properly implement and maintain this?

If the answer to any of these is "no," it's probably not worth adding. And I don't.

Train Your Team in MVF Principles

As you bring on team members, explicitly train them in your simplicity-focused approach. Otherwise, they may bring complexity from previous roles. Share this book with them. Make simplification a core value. Recognize and reward team members who find ways to streamline processes.

Embracing Gradual Growth

Perhaps the most important scaling principle is patience. Sustainable growth happens gradually, not overnight. I've seen many businesses falter by trying to grow too quickly - hiring too many people, launching too many products, or expanding to too many channels at once.

The businesses that succeed long-term typically focus on 20-30% annual growth - enough to be meaningful but not so much that their systems and culture break under pressure. As one of my mentors told me early in my career...

"It's better to grow steadily for ten years than to explode for one year and burn out."

7

In Conclusion

Implementation is the ONLY superpower you need to succeed.

We've come a long way.

You've made it to the end of our journey together. Throughout this book, we've explored how to strip away unnecessary complexity from your marketing and build a Minimum Viable Funnel™ that actually works.

We began by looking at the evolution of marketing funnels, from their simple beginnings to the overly complex systems many struggle with today. We explored why most complex funnels fail and why simplicity often leads to better results.

Then we dug deep into my SEED Marketing™ Model, giving you a framework to create content that positions you as an expert, engages your audience, echoes your values, and delivers real transformation.

We moved beyond traditional lead generation, and I hope you can now see how to attract buyers instead of freebie hunters and build a list of customers rather than just subscribers.

With the Minimum Viable Funnel™ Framework, you learned the essential components of a streamlined marketing system that converts without complexity, adding in Selling Without Selling™ that gave you a conversational framework to close sales without feeling pushy or manipulative.

Then, to finish, we explored how to scale your success while maintaining the simplicity that makes your business effective and enjoyable to run.

The path I've laid out isn't just theoretical. It's built on years of hands-on experience helping hundreds of clients simplify their marketing and grow their businesses.

I've seen it work across industries, business models, and at various stages of business growth.

But a book can only take you so far. Transformation happens when you take action.

I encourage you to visit the resources page **www.simplifythefunnel.com/resources** for additional tools, templates, and guides to help you implement what you've learned.

If you're looking for more guidance and support as you implement these strategies, I invite you to explore...

SIMPLIFY BUSINESS ACADEMY

The Only System That Turns Marketing Complexity Into Predictable Profit - Without The Tech Headaches or Content Creation That Gets Ignored

You can become part of a community of entrepreneurs who finally create a profitable online business in 90 days - even after wasting thousands of dollars and years of effort on complicated marketing systems that never delivered.

You can view all the information about the academy by scanning this QR code or by visiting www.simplifybusinessacademy.com

The academy is where I take everything you've learned in this book to the next level, with comprehensive training, implementation support, and a community of like-minded entrepreneurs who are all focused on simplification.

There will be another live cohort starting again very soon,

but you can access the full training library, members area and community right away - then pick the date to join the live group calls that works best for you.

Remember...

Implementation is the ONLY superpower you need to succeed.

The strategies in this book work - but only if you put them into practice.

Start small. Pick one area to simplify first. See the results. Then move on to the next. Before long, you'll have a streamlined, effective marketing system that brings in consistent leads and sales without overwhelming you.

Thank you for joining me on this journey toward simplification. I truly believe that by simplifying your marketing, you'll not only grow your business but also reclaim the freedom and fulfillment that probably led you to start your business in the first place.

This book has been a labor of love, and it's been many years in the making. On honored to have been able to write this, get it published, and get it in your hands to help you simplify not only your funnel but your business as a whole.

ANT HODGES

Here's to your success with simple, effective marketing!

Ant Hodges

As a final thought... I'd love to hear about your success with the MVF. Connect with me on social media @AntHodges (Instagram is my playground) or email your story service@hodgesnet.com. Your experiences might help other entrepreneurs find the courage to simplify their own marketing.

About the author Ant Hodges

Ant Hodges is an innovative leader in the online marketing space, known for turning complex marketing funnels into simple, effective systems. With two decades of experience, he has built a reputation as a trusted marketing coach, strategist, and author who delivers results without the usual overwhelm.

WWW.SIMPLIFYTHEFUNNEL.COM

Starting his career in 2007, Ant co-founded a UK branding and advertising agency that quickly grew into a multi-six-figure operation serving notable clients in education, government, and the non-profit sector. Navigating the challenges of the late-2000s recession taught him a fundamental truth that defines his approach today...

Success in marketing doesn't require complexity - it requires clarity, human connection, and focus on unchanging psychological principles.

At the core of Ant's methodology is his **Minimum Viable Funnel™** (MVF) framework, which focuses on building only the essential components needed to drive sales. By rejecting complexity and embracing a "minimum viable" approach, his clients routinely reach six-figure revenues in a fraction of the time typically required.

His battle-tested systems include the **SEED Marketing™** model (Shaping expert content, Engaging authentically, Echoing core values, and Delivering actionable value) and the **Selling Without Selling™** methodology - practical frameworks that help entrepreneurs attract loyal customers without manipulation or high pressure tactics.

What truly distinguishes Ant is his approach to helping others replicate his success. After applying his own principles to build a seven-figure online business (earning him Kajabi's Millionaire Hero Award in 2022), he now shares these strategies through keynote presentations across Europe, North America, and Asia.

Ant is passionate about changing the "hustle culture" narrative for online business owners. When others glorify 24/7 work and endless tactics, he champions a counterintuitive truth:

Simplicity, connection, and quality will outperform frantic hustle every time.

This philosophy has helped hundreds of entrepreneurs achieve greater results with less stress, often rediscovering the freedom that inspired them to start their businesses in the first place.

With a track record of client success and a dedication to cutting through hype, Ant remains committed to helping entrepreneurs "simplify the funnel" and build sustainable businesses without overwhelm.

Connect with Ant:

Instagram: @AntHodges
Email: service@hodgesnet.com
Website: www.anthodges.com

Printed in Dunstable, United Kingdom

71100842R00143